8/8/2024

Steps to Composition

(Development of Writing Skill, from Primary to Secondary Level)Part-1, Includes Picture Composition, Essay & Story Writing

Mr. Peter

First Edition- September 2022
Second Edition- October 2023
Last Modified- 08-08-2024

Published in association with Amazon, Notion Press, and Google.

https://kdp.amazon.com/en_US/ & https://notionpress.com/

DEDICATION

The book is dedicated to all those children who, like Peter, are afraid of composing, whether writing a paragraph or a story and love to give a suitable excuse for the reason.

Description of the Book

Mr. Peter's **'Advanced Writing Skill, the Complete Version'** consists of three Parts **(Part 1, Part 2 & Part 3).**
The book is Mr. Peter's attempt to include all necessary writing skills and methods suitable for students of all standards, from Primary to higher secondary level. The book includes the methods of writing skills as described below-

Part 1, "Steps to Composition (Development of Writing Skill, from Primary to Secondary Level)," includes all types of paragraph writing, essay writing, picture story composition, and story writing with titles and morals where applicable. The book includes paragraphs and essays on eminent personalities, famous places, animals, and things, narrating personal experiences, slogans, and occasions.
Thus, they verge from autobiographical to biographical, narrative, and descriptive writing, including Picture Story Composition separately.

"Development of Writing Skill, Part-2" includes mainly **Letter Writing**, dividing it firstly into two heads: **Formal** & **Informal**; then sub-dividing each one into further sub-heads as—**business letters**, including advertisements, inquiries, replies, placing an order, letters of complaint, **application for jobs—letters to the editor**—letters to **Institutional Heads**, like Principal, Headmaster— to **Municipal Commissioner, Chairman, Mayor**—to **bank authorities**—different official & unofficial **Invitations** and **Replies**—and the **Informal letters**; as to friends, relatives, acquittances and parents.

The 3rd book in the series of Writing Skills, i.e., "Development of Writing Skill, Part-3," includes all other remaining important sections of writing skills or composition, which are necessary for practice by students and learners. Thus, the book includes- **E-mails, Poster Making, Notices, Processing, Dialogue, Articles, Speech & Debate Writing, Diary entries, Summaries, and Reporting for school newsletters and Newspapers** with ample examples for study and exercises.

CONTENTS

ACKNOWLEDGMENTS

For the section of Peter's **'Picture Composition'** in part 1, Mr. Peter was directly inspired by the book published by UpToSchoolWorksheets for the Nursery level. However, the book's essence is written differently and developed by Mr. Peter himself.

Besides, *f*or images, Mr. Peter humbly pays tribute to free online images that he had searched through search engines Bing, Google, Micro Soft Stock Images, and others. However, if any issue arises regarding using images under anyone's right, Peter ensures that such is deleted immediately from his book.
Without data and information, a book is always incomplete and impossible. Some books are based on research. However, this one does not belong to that group. It is mainly based on information and data, which, in many cases, Mr. Peter gathers from Encyclopedia Britannica, en.wikipedia.org, solarsystem.nasa.gov, and Google. For this, Mr. Peter pays his humble tribute to those and likes to give thanks to thousands of contributors.

1. INTRODUCTION

What do we mean by **'writing skill'** or **'composition'**?

'Writing Skill' is the 'ability to write about something,' that is, to expand or express a thought about an incident, event, or situation, including picture description in words or lines; the skill includes paragraph writing, letter writing, email writing, notice writing, poster making, etc.

'Composition' means 'organizing different parts or facts' (i.e., ideas, concepts of pictures, or a particular incident) to give a structure,' *a complete thought*. So, it also denotes the same thing, '**the art of writing.'**

Therefore, the **'Picture Composition'** means, as already said or given hint, '*Organizing different parts* (**read:** ideas or thoughts of a particular picture or pictures) *to give a complete idea* or *thought about different parts of the picture or pictures given in written form* of sentences or paragraph.
The writer may invent the thought given in his imagination (by organizing the sequence of events or picture parts given) to entertain us. So, it is also called **'Picture Story Composition'**.

Before going to the main chapter, let's discuss some more of the meanings of different terms, used in writing skills, such as,

A. **Picture Composition:** As already introduced and discussed above, *picture composition involves giving a picture or several pictures; the learner has to develop them into a story, write some lines, or form a paragraph.*
   It should be noted that such ones are suitable for students of standard 1 to 5, i.e., for the students of the Primary Level.

B. **Paragraph Writing — (Descriptive or Narrative):** It is *a piece of writing that* usually consists of several (more than two but not very many) sentences ***dealing with a single subject*** (i.e., topic) given or chosen. Thus, single or double-sentence writing can't be termed as a paragraph. However, it can be treated so, as a separate paragraph if that is itself a part of an essay or a story where many paragraphs are included. So, a paragraph is merely **'the combination of some lines or sentences in text** (from three to many, but not very much in quantity).

Note: ***Several means 'more than two, but not very many' sentences***.

When a paragraph tends to be very long, we include or divide it into others at a point where discussion may take a turn. This is called 'Essay Writing.'

C. **Essay Writing:**—The piece of writing, which generally consists of several (more than two but not very many) paragraphs ***dealing with a single subject matter*** (i.e., topic) given or chosen, ***but has several turns of discussion in it***. (i.e., an essay is *an explanation of an idea* that is expressed *through different paragraphs (generally* *more than two).* In an essay, a writer presents his/her opinion with supporting examples to prove his or her point and persuade the readers to accept it.

- An essay has three main parts: **Introduction, Body,** and **Conclusion.**
- In the Introduction, we introduce the topic with Question statements—who, what, why, when, etc.
- Thus, we present some ***statistics*** as well as ***facts*** and ***detailed data***.
- We also give interesting points that contribute to different sides of the topic.
- We may use '***Proverbs***' and '***Idioms***' to make writing more creative and expressive.

Thus, paragraph and essay writing are almost the same, dealing with a single subject matter (i.e., one topic) that is based on fact, not imaginary; the difference lies only in the length of the composition: one is composed of ***several sentences, and another consists of several paragraphs***.

An essay includes a paragraph where the discussion takes a turn, dealing with different sides or points of the same topic (i.e., subject matter).

D. The paragraph and **essay writing:**

- A paragraph and an essay are both writing pieces dealing with a single subject matter that is based on fact or truth, not imagination.
- A paragraph consists of several sentences (more than two), whereas, an essay consists of several paragraphs. The difference lies in length only.
- An Essay must include several paragraphs in it, generally from ***three to many***.
- Another important thing is that both types of writing have different manners. For example, a paragraph may be 'descriptive' or 'narrative'; similarly, an essay also has different manners. Thus, it may be of ***different kinds, more than two***.

For examinations, essays are common in elementary, middle, high school, and college; one may even need to write essays in business. It is essential, as it is a writing piece that expresses both **information and the writer's opinion.**" It includes the author's own argument. However, the definition is vague, overlapping with those of a paper, an article, a pamphlet, and a short story (because they also include information and the author's opinion, directly and indirectly). **Essays** have traditionally been sub-classified as **formal** and **informal,** like letter writing.

How to write an Essay:

For some, writing an essay is as simple as sitting down with their pen and copybook or before the computer and beginning to type, but for a lot, it needs study and planning to arrange the ideas about the topic chosen and given. It may include research and sorting out into paragraphs. However, generally, an essay includes the following:

There are seven steps for writing a successful essay:

1) Pick a topic.
2) Prepare an outline or diagram of your ideas about the topic chosen or given.
3) Write a suitable title for the essay.
4) Write an introduction as a paragraph with some sentences.
5) Develop or elaborate your thesis ('thesis' means ' the notion, theory or idea about the topic, made or thought of'). This is also called the 'body' of the essay.

6) The essay's body may consist of more than one paragraph. Thus, from single to many.
7) Write a conclusion in a separate paragraph.

Kinds Of Essay Writing: Essays are of several kinds, which are as follows:

- **Descriptive Essays:** Tell a story or impart information about the topic using descriptive words, such as shape, size, age, and time.
- **Narrative Essays:** Focus on the details of the events, situation, experience, slogans, etc., including the writer's opinion over the point.
- **Persuasive Essay:** An essay that convinces the readers about a viewpoint supporting or against someone or something.
- **Comparative Essay:** Comparing two or more different things, embedding the author's opinions.
- **Expository Essay:** This type of essay explains to readers how to complete a given process. It includes different steps to move on. Give step-by-step instructions.

For academic purposes, a student needs to know each kind of writing skill. However, **Descriptive** and **Narrative** essays are the most common and popular for students.

E. Descriptive Writing:

- Descriptive writing describes a person, place, thing, or animal.
- In descriptive writing, we often use descriptive words (adjectives to describe different nouns or pronouns) that may include shapes, likes, dislikes, sizes, colors, habits, etc.
- Descriptive writings on people or persons are mostly biographical sketches of the person from birth to the present, which may include their achievements, works, and contributions and highlight significant events in their lives.
- The sketch (the description of personalities and qualities) may be written by the author (if so, it is called 'autobiographical'); if by any other person than he or she, it is merely 'biographical writing.'

  Essay writing in person—may be biographical and autobiographical (when 'descriptive').

F. Narrative Writing:

- Narrative writing involves details of an event, experience, or_***happening in a person's life***.
- The literary forms such as **novels** and **short stories** are explicit narratives told by the narrator.
- Narrative writing informs us about events, characters, occasions, slogans, and even proverbs that may affect a person's life or society as a whole.
- Till the end, narrative writing sustains the reader's interest, and thus, detective stories, thriller writings, diary writing, essays, reporting, stories, novels, etc., belong to the group of narrative writing.

G. Story Writing:

Storywriting is an art and the oldest form of written composition. It is generally a **work of imagination** written in an easily understandable grammatical structure. A short story is meant to be read in a single sitting, so it should be as **direct and brief** as possible.

A short story is **a fictional work of prose** that is ***much shorter in length than a novel***.

In his essay 'The Philosophy of Composition,' Edgar Allan Poe said a short story should be read in one sitting.

A short story usually **focuses on one plot, one main character** (with a few additional minor characters), and **one central theme** (*whereas a novel takes multiple plots and themes to deal with, with various prominent characters to elaborate on*).

Main points related to story writing:

- **Must have a Title:** The story's title must be engaging and *evoke curiosity*.
- A planned and logical series of events must be reflected in the story, and the events should not deviate from its central theme.
- There must be an exciting theme in the story, which is the controlling idea of the story.
- The depiction of the characters must be engaging and convincing.
- The language of the story must suit it and be appropriate for its setting.
- Many stories also convey a moral lesson at the end.

2. PICTURE STORY COMPOSITION (Primary Level)

Let's begin with 'Picture Story Composition.' This section is designed to develop a student's writing skills, from Single Sentence Formation to Paragraph Writing. After each step, there is also an answer guide for beginners.

In Picture Composition, a picture or some pictures are given; the learner is asked to develop them into a story or write some lines or a paragraph.

Guidelines for writing good picture composition:

1) Look at the picture carefully.
2) Note down points of what you see in every part of the picture.
3) Ask questions based on these points, like *what or who is present there*, *what is happening*, *what are they doing*, etc.

You may use the answers to such questions to make a paragraph.

STEP-1 (Single to Double Sentence Writing)

1. Beginner's Single Sentences: (suitable for standard-1)

Complete the sentences based on the pictures given:

This is a ________. (book)
That is a ________. (ball)

She is my ……………. (mom)
He is my ___________. (dad)

The girl is my ________. (sister)
The boy is my ________. (brother)

The girl is ……………………………… (talking over phone)
The man is ___________________________. (reading a book.)

The girls are ……………….. (talking)

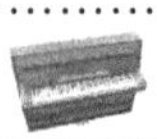

The boys are _________________________music. (playing)

The birds are _______________________ in the sky. (flying)

The wolves are ……………………………….. (howling)

The dog is ___________________________.

The boy is ___________________________.

2. Single Sentence Writing with Options: (Primary Level, Standard 1 to 5)

Complete the sentences based on options, given in pictures: (by using naming, describing or doing words as necessary.)

The baby birds are feeling ___________, because ______________________________

Answer guide:

a) *happy, their parents are returning.*
b) *happy, the mother bird is feeding them.*
c) *excited, the day is breaking.*

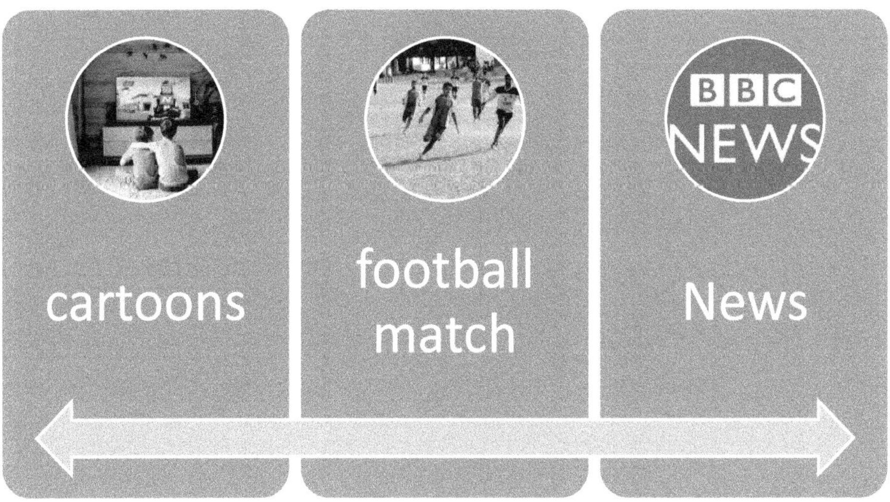

I would like to see ___________, because ____________________________________

Answer guide:

a) *cartoons, these are entertaining.*
b) *football match, it is thrilling.*
c) *news, it enriches my knowledge of the world.*

For picnic I like to go __________, because ______________________________

Answer guide:

a) *on a beach, I love sunsets over the seas.*
b) *a zoo, I come to know of different animals and birds as well.*
c) *hills, because it is cool to see the sunrise over the peaks.*

= ___________ is my favorite season, because _____________________________

Answer guide:

a) *Rainy season, it is refreshing, and nature grows green around.*
b) *Winter season, ice fall around and I love skating.*
c) *Spring, nature becomes colorful all around and we can see different flowers in our garden.*

play with a pet

bathe a pet

watch tv with a pet

If I had a pet, I would ....

Answer guide:

a) play with it.
b) bathe it every day.
c) watch tv sitting beside it.

3. Two or More sentences with examples (Primary Level, Standard 1 To 5)

Read the sentences about the picture on the left. Then write two or more sentences for each about the pictures, given next:

Table-1

Maizie is going to school.
She walks to school every day.

Write two or more sentences against the picture.
1. ____
2. ____

Anna is riding a cycle. (write more two sentences)
1. ____
2. ____

Table-2

Pizza is a junk food. We should not __________.
We should not eat it everyday.

Write two or more sentences against the picture.
1. ______________________________
2. ______________________________

There are fruits. (write more two sentences)
1. ______________________________
2. ______________________________

Table-3

Archie is a careless boy. One day, he threw ___ .
A man ______________________________.

1. ______________________________
2. ______________________________

1. ______________________________
2. ______________________________

Table-4

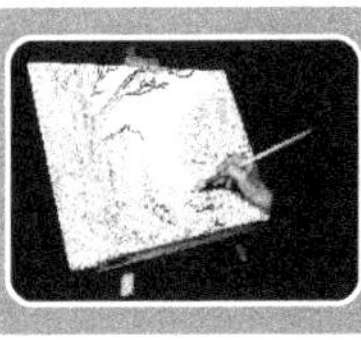

Elias likes to draw paint. He just finished ________.

It is about ______________________________ .

Write two sentences against the picture

1. ____

2. ____

Leon sits before a piano. (write two more)

1. ____

2. ____

Table-5

Sonny is swimming in a river.

Swimming is good for health.

1. ____

2. ____

1. ____

2. ____

Answer Guide

Answer guide of the above tables (students' answers may vary, and that should always be welcomed):

1.

(a) I wash my hands daily before and after my meal. I use hand washing to wash my hands. It is hygienic for health.

(b) Anna loves cycling every day. She is going to her friend Alisha.

2.

(a) Pizza is a junk food. We should not eat it every day. It is harmful to our health.

(b) Milk is a healthy drink. Ember drinks two glasses of milk every day.

(c) Anna loves fruits. However, cherries are her favorite.

3.

(a) Archie is a careless boy. One day, he threw a banana peel on the road. A man stepped on it. He slipped and fell down. The man got hurt on his knees and the elbow of his right hand.

(b) Tom is a nice guy. He collects used bottles every Friday to keep his locality clean.

(c) Alisha is a good girl. She is helping her mother with her cooking.

4.

(a) Elias likes to draw paint. He just finished his paintings. It is about a tree and green grass beside a village.

(b) Little Dean likes his dolls. He fell asleep while playing with them on the lawn.

(c) Leon is now in a music class. He is playing the piano on a popular song.

5.

(a) Elias is running with a football. He is quite good at playing football and wants to be an international player one day.

(b) Anna is a good girl. She is now doing her homework. After that, she likes to read a story of fairy tales.

STEP-2 (Writing Three or More Sentences, Using Clues)

4. Writing a short paragraph in three or more sentences (Primary Level, Standard 2 to 5)

Write three or more sentences *using the clues* given based on the pictures. (However, regarding points or clues, a learner is free to use his or her own)

Table-1

best friends, do everything together, different hobbies

- Finn & John are two best friends.
- They read & play together.
- However, they have different hobbies.
- Finn likes swimming, when John likes to play bad-minton.

green plants, yellow carrot, important source of vitamins and minerals. good for eyes and skin.

- ______
- ______
- ______

colorful umbrella, looks attractive, protects from heat and rain.

- ______
- ______
- ______

Table-2

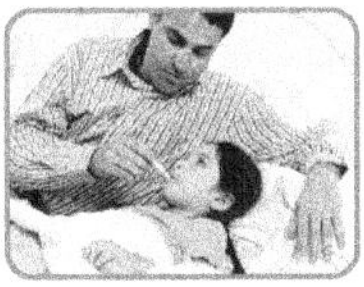

sick, resting in bed, did not go to school for three days.

- ______________________________
- ______________________________
- ______________________________

horse cart, farmer taking hay, going to sell in the market.

- ______________________________
- ______________________________
- ______________________________

green bus, traveling together, great fun

- ______________________________
- ______________________________
- ______________________________

Table-3

father's office bag, grey, black zips, carrying documents and paper in it

- ______________________________
- ______________________________
- ______________________________

a red boat, floating on a river, carries passengers and goods, used for short distances.

- ______________________________
- ______________________________
- ______________________________

tortoise, happy, hard shell, walks slow, lives longer than human.

- ______________________________
- ______________________________
- ______________________________

Table-4

deer, lives on grass, lives in forest, runs very fast.

- ______________________________
- ______________________________
- ______________________________

pet dogs, different in color, different species in the world, layal and faithfull animal among all.

- ______________________________
- ______________________________
- ______________________________

horse, four strong legs, beautiful crest upon the neck, many love horse riding.

- ______________________________
- ______________________________
- ______________________________

Table-5

my father, my best friend, love father, takes care.

- ______________________________
- ______________________________
- ______________________________

good friends like stars, do many things together, support us when we are sad.

- ______________________________
- ______________________________
- ______________________________

wake up at 5 a.m., brush teeth, study till 9 a.m., getting ready for school, a daily routine

- ______________________________
- ______________________________
- ______________________________

Table-6

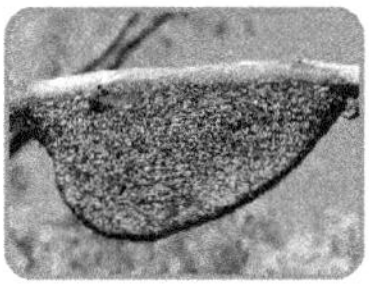

honeybee, collect nectar from flowers and store in hundred rooms, called honeycomb.

- ______________________________
- ______________________________
- ______________________________

Felix, a god boy, helps father, cleaning house & others.

- ______________________________
- ______________________________
- ______________________________

Leon, a good boy, loves study, has learnt many things, won competitions.

- ______________________________
- ______________________________
- ______________________________

Answer Guide to

best friends—carrots—umbrella—when you are sick—horse cart—green bus—father's office bag—boat on a river—tortoise—deer—pet dog—horse—about your father—good friends—daily routine—honey bee & honeycomb—cleaning your house & its surrounding—when you love your study;

Answer guides are only for assistance and giving learners information. Encourage your kids to write as many sentences as she/he can using the points or points thought of yourself in order to develop his or her writing skills. (Students' answers may vary, and that should be welcomed):

(1)

a) Finn and John are best friends. They read and play together. However, they have different hobbies. Finn likes swimming, while John likes to play badminton.

b) Carrots are yellow in color, but their plants are green like others. Carrots are an important source of vitamins and minerals. One who drinks half a cup of carrot juice every day hardly suffers from eye and skin disease.

c) Jacob has an umbrella. It is not colorful like Alisha's. An umbrella is a very useful instrument when it rains. It protects us from the scorching heat of the sun in summer and rain in the rainy season.

(2)

(a) Sabine is a little girl. She has been sick for a few days. The doctor has asked her to take bed rest. She is resting in her bed. She did not go to school today.

(b) A Horse cart is a horse-drawn vehicle. It is pulled by one or a team of horses. It is widely used in villages or the countryside. A farmer uses a horse cart to take hay or sacks of corn from one place to another. A horse cart also goes to the market to sell corn.

(c) Bus is a common transport means on land. We travel on a bus to school every day. A lot of my classmates travel also on this bus. We have so much fun traveling together. I love the song 'Wheels on the Bus.' That was green in color.

(3)

(a) This is a picture of my father's grey office bag. It has many black zips and pockets, where he carries his important documents and papers.
(b) There is a red boat on the river. A boat effortlessly floats on water. Many boats have engines. However, many others move on oars. Boats carry passengers and goods to reach them for a short distance.
(c) Tortoises belong to reptiles. It has hard shells. The hard shell protects it from outward threats. Tortoises can vary in size. Some swim best, others generally walk. They walk very slowly, and they always look happy. A tortoise lives longer than animals around us and even longer than human beings.

(4)

(a) Deer are mammals like cows, elephants, and human beings. They live on green grass and in jungles. A male deer is called a buck, and a female deer is called a doe. However, some larger males are referred to as stags and female deer of the species are known as hinds. A young deer is called a fawn. Deer can jump up to 10 feet high, and they are very good swimmers, too. They are good runners on grass or land.

More about Deer:

(Deer are the only group of animals in the world with antlers. Antlers are the fastest-growing living tissue in the world! Each year, antlers fall off and regrow. There are over 60 different species of deer worldwide. Deer are present on all continents except Antarctica. All species of deer have antlers, with few exceptions, like the Chinese water deer.)

(b) Dogs are faithful and loyal animals. They become pets too quickly. There are different species of dogs worldwide, and they are different in size and color. Dogs' sense of smell is at least 40 times better than ours. Some dogs are incredible swimmers, and they can run very fast on land. Dogs have fewer holes in their skin, so they don't sweat like us.

(c) A horse is a domesticated animal like a cow or goat. A horse is an odd-toed and hooped mammal. A horse has four strong legs, and they can run very fast. Horses are highly intelligent animals. And it is an animal that can sleep standing up. A male horse has 40 teeth, while a mare (a female horse) has only 36. Another important fact about horses is that they can't breathe through the mouth like us, except through the nose. Horses are used for riding and transport. Some people have also kept horses as their pets since earlier days.

(5)

(a) Parents, a father and mother, are the most loving and caring persons in a family. Every mother and father cares for his or her child dearly and to the best of their capacity. However, I love my father most. He is the most dutiful person. He meets all my demands and takes care of my studies. I believe him to be an intelligent person, too. He answers all my questions as well. He is my best friend, guide, and philosopher. I love my father very much.
(b) Friends is the other name of love and trust. I am lucky that I have friends. Pitt and Tom are my best friends. We play together and share often our Tiffin. They are my stars. When I feel sad, they visit me and I feel happy once again playing with them.

(c) I am Shreya. I read in class 2. I am an early riser. I wake up 5 a.m. every morning and walk with my father for half an hour after brush my teeth and face wash. From 7 to 9 a.m. I study and then gets ready for my school which sits at 10 a.m. From Monday to Friday, it is my daily routine. On Saturday & Sunday I have lot of fun. Sometimes, I also play video games.

(6)

(a) Honey bees belong to the family of insects. Honey bees are tiny insects. They are little yellow and black insects with wings and sharp stings, which we always fear! Generally, honey bees live in grasslands, forests, and gardens. However, recently, they have reared for economic importance. Honey bees collect nectar from flowers. From nectar, honey bees make honey and store that in hundreds of beehives. When the beehives are filled with honey, we call it a honeycomb. Men collect honey for their use from these honeycombs. It is of great economic importance to the human world.

(b) Felix is a good boy. He reads in class 2. However, he often helps his father clean the house and its surroundings. Felix and his family know the best way to live healthily is to live in a clean home. Cleaning floors, kitchen, bathroom, and many others regularly eliminates germs, dirt, and dust and protects us from falling sick. We do not suffer from allergies and infections. Besides, housecleaning improves one's confidence levels and self-esteem, which also helps to acquire respect from others.

(c) Leon is a good boy. He loves to study, and this habit has led him to learn many things beyond his school syllabus. Besides securing good marks in his examinations, Leon has participated in many competitions and won medals.

STEP-3 (Writing Short Paragraphs, Using Clues)

5. Write short paragraphs against the pictures given, in 60 words only. You may use the clues given in the first line. However, you are free to use your own:

Table-1

Ship: *white color, goes on seas and oceans, travel long distances)*

I can see a ship with white sails in the picture. A ship is a large watercraft that travels long distances on seas and oceans, as opposed to a boat which is a smaller watercraft to travel short distances in river. A ship carries passengers as well as cargos from one country to another. In earlier time, ships mainly floated on using sails and paddles. However, in modern time it floats and moves on engine.

The sun: rise in the east--warmth pleasant--a star--gives energy

____

____

____

____

Table-2

A wood house with straw roofs--cool inside--plan to grow garden:

____

____

____

____

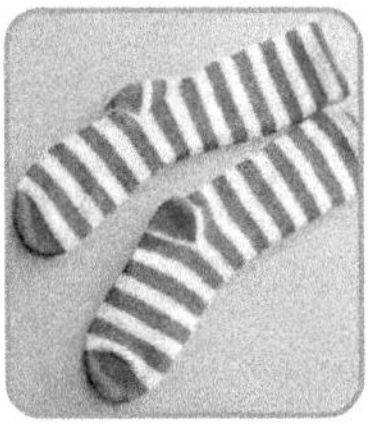

Socks: purple color with white stripes--long legs--wear while playing football

____

____

____

____

Table-3

Write a paragraph on cupboard in your house: neat and clean clothes, hang shirts & pants in it, pillows kept on shelf, socks and other small things in drawe.

____

____

____

____

Gardening: flower plants from nursery, flowerpots, digging, watering, etc.

____

____

____

____

Table-4

Divya practices archery daily--exercises to stay fit--good aim--wants to go for Olympics one day

____

____

____

____

John is ambitious to be a great basket ball player:

____

____

____

____

Table-5

Little Sumi likes to read stories:buy books and colect from library too, sometimes exchange books with her friends.

____

____

____

____

Write a paragraph on your parents: (loving, caring, supporting, mention their profession, etc.

____

____

____

____

Table-6

Playing Chess: 8*8 square board with 16 pieces for each, have different styles of movement, an internationally played indoor game, develop persistence, patience & concentration

____

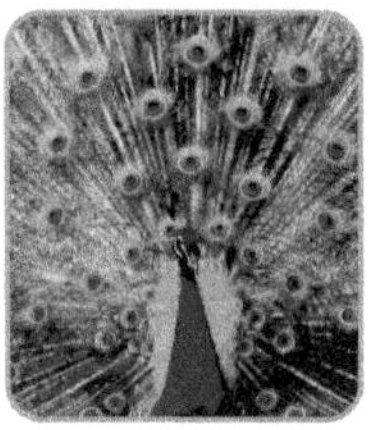

Peacock: largest & heaviset bird with a crown on head & dazzling colorful feathers, national bird in India

____

Table-7

Cooking: an art, need for healthy life, everyone should learn

____

Washing Clothes: bucket, water, detergent, dip clothes, scrub, rinse & dry

____

Answer Guide to

Ships—the Sun—wood house—socks—a cupboard in your house—gardening—Archery as your hobby—Playing basketball—reading story books—your parents—playing chess—peacock—cooking—washing clothes.

(Encourage your kids to innovate her or his clues, and let her or him write as many sentences as far as s/he can. **That is good to develop his or her writing skills without restrictions.** The answer guide is provided only to add information and help the student)**:**

(1)

(b) We **get up early** every day when the sun rises in the east. The sun glows in the east sky with yellow color, and its warmth is so pleasant and uplifting. The sun is a star in the center of the solar system. We are alive because of the sun. It gives us light, heat, and energy to move and work. The food that we consume is produced in the presence of sunlight. If there is no sun, no animal exists on the planet.

(2)

(a) Anita is **my best friend**. She lives in a house made of wood with a straw roof. It is cool inside. Anita and her parents love to grow a garden in front of their house. I helped them with baby flower plants from my parents' nursery. I love to visit Anita's house often and play together for hours.

(b) These are my **new pair of socks**, which my mother bought for me yesterday. They are purple with white stripes and do not have a shade like my earlier ones. They also have long legs. I like to wear them when I play football, and I wear a white pair when I go to school every day.

(3)

(a) You can see my **cupboard** here. There, I keep only my neat and clean clothes. My shirts and pants hang on hangers. Two pillows, too, are kept on the shelf. The small things, like socks, hand gloves, and ties, are neatly folded and kept in the drawers.

(b) **Gardening** is growing and cultivating plants, sometimes as a hobby and often as an economic activity to gain profits.
Peter likes gardening. He has a garden in front of his house. He collects flower plants from a local nursery. He uses some brown or colored pots. However, Peter prefers to plant them more on open ground than in small pots. He digs and adds some natural fertilizers before planting a plant. Peter's children water them every day when it is not the rainy season.

(4)

(a) **Divya** is a little girl in class VII. She likes archery very much. She practices it every day and also exercises to keep fit. Divya has a good aim in her archery. She has already won many school prizes and two medals at the district level. Divya wants to play in the Olympics one day.

(b) **Basketball** is a great way to exercise and have fun with friends. **I** started playing basketball when I was a kid. Now, I am a class VII student and play basketball for my school team. We have already won a few prizes since last year. Playing basketball requires a ton of stamina and a vast amount of energy, like playing football. It is an exercise. It keeps us fit and healthy. Like any other outdoor game, this game can bring us joy and foster better friendships among players.

(5)

(a) **Little Sumi likes to read stories** very much. For this, her father has bought her many storybooks from shopkeepers. Little Sumi also collects some books from the library in her locality. Some friends also like to read stories. Little Sumi often exchanges books with them.

(b) **My parents** are my strength to move on. I read in class V, and I love them very much. Perhaps no child does not love his or her parents. They support us in more ways than we can count. My father is a schoolteacher, and he helps me with my studies. My mother is a doctor, and I have learned patience from my mom. My parents have two kids, I am, and my little sister, Edith.

(6)

(a) Different games help us to develop different aptitudes and skills. **Chess** is an internationally played game in the category of indoor games. The play of chess develops persistence, patience, and concentration. Chess is an 8 x 8 square board game played between two players. The chess consists of 2 sets of colored pieces, white and black. Each set has 16 pieces: precisely eight pawns, two bishops, two knights, two rooks, one queen, and one king. Different types of pieces have different styles of movement. Pawns have the least power, while the queen holds the maximum power. I love playing chess. My father was my first master. I learned to play chess from him. It can also be played on a computer or mobile nowadays. However, I like to play it with my friends.

(b) **Peacock** is the largest and heaviest bird that can fly, though not so high in the sky. It has a small mouth and a vast body. The weight of the **peacock** is about 5 to 10 kg. A peacock has a crown and a long, gleaming dark blue neck. It has gorgeous feathers in a variety of colors. When it dances in the rain, spreading its all-feathers round, rippling, and its beauty instantly brings comfort to our eyes. For its magnificent beauty and significant religious involvement in Bharatiya traditions, the bird is considered as the National Bird of Bharat.

(7)

(a) **Cooking** is an art that everybody should learn. Without cooked food, a human being can't live a healthy life. Cooking is required to make food edible and tasty, which makes us happy and healthy. I do cook, for I love having food. However, I can't cook as well as my mother does. But I can say that my cooking is good enough for me to invite my friends often and have a lot of fun with them.

(b) We need to **wash our clothes** every day. It keeps us fit and healthy, and we can avoid many diseases using clean clothes. However, washing clothes includes the following steps.

- Step 1: Take a bucket and fill it with water;
- Step 2: Add Detergent, mix well, and dip your dirty clothes into the water;
- Step 3: leave for twenty to thirty minutes;
- Step 4: Scrubbed thoroughly one by one, and wash the clothes in fresh and clean water twice;
- Step 5: Rinse and dry;
- Step 6: Press and fold your clothes properly;
- Step 7: They are now ready to be used again.

STEP-4 (Writing Paragraphs, Without Clues)

(1) Carefully read the pictures given. Write short paragraphs within 100 words:

A Park

Important points to remember: Think about the different parts or points of the picture. Think properly and express them in sentences. Read one example:

park

butterfly

rabbits

birds

Try to give answers to the questions:

- What is the album about? Is this of a park, garden, forest, or any other?
- What can be seen in different frames and think them to be in one place.
- Is there any bird, any other animal, man or butterflies?
- Are there any flowers in the picture? And of what color?
- Try to recognize anything beyond these.

If we write the answers together:

This is a sight of a park where birds, flowers, and butterflies can be seen along with some rabbits and guinea pigs. Many long and large trees are also found in some parks. Here, there are a lot of birds, rabbits, and flowers of different colors. They are seen in different frames of the album. Some birds are sitting on a high perch of a tree. A cluster of flowers is hanging from the high branches of the trees. Some rabbits are on the grounds, collecting their food or playing together. A butterfly of orange and black color is also seen resting on some buds.

Mother Birds

(2) Look at the picture carefully and write seven sentences about it.

Mother birds always love their babies unconditionally. They spend a lot of time taking care of their babies and keeping them safe. Baby birds always depend on their parents to eat food. In this case, a mother bird usually digests the food and then puts that food into the babies' mouth. The babies always open their mouths wide and screech for food when they are hungry. The mother birds often feed their babies insects so that they can get more protein and grow healthy.

Birthday Party

(3) Look at the picture carefully, and try to point out things to write about them in simple sentences.

Every year I celebrate my birthday on 30th July and my elder brother's on 2nd December. However, this is my cousin's Lucy. We reached there in time. We wished her saying in rhythm and jointly 'Happy Birth Day to You', "Many, Many Returns of the Day', etc. We recited some other verses too together. Lucy served us with delicious cake which her aunt had baked, and her mother had prepared mouth-watering dishes for all of us attended in the party on that day. We celebrate the party with great joy and excitement together. **However, you may begin with:** I am Lucy. I am five years old and I read in standard III.

Classroom

(4) Look at the picture carefully, and write seven sentences about it.

My classroom is full of happy memories. We study there and play together after each period over. Though our classroom is small, we love it dearly. Our classroom has several desks, a chair, and a table for our teacher. The teachers love us and take care. During Tiffin time, we have our Tiffin, but the best thing is to play together in the playground.

Flying Kite

(5) Look at the given pictures. Write three short paragraphs about what you think may have happened. Remember to write a title to your paragraphs.

Raju woke up early. It was a clear, sunny day—a perfect day to fly his kite. He went to a park near his house.

The wind was favorable, and his kite went up high in the sky. Raju was feeling excited. Slowly, a strong breeze blew his kite towards a tall tree, and it got stuck in the branches. Raju tried hard to get his kite out of the tree but could not. He had no more kites to fly, so he finally returned home.

Good Habits

(6) The pictures below show some good habits every child must learn. **Write a short paragraph on good habits** with the help of the visual stimulus given below.

It is said that **going to bed early makes a man healthy, wealthy, and wise.** Going to bed early and waking up early is a good habit. A habit means repetition of the same action. Other habits like brushing our teeth, bathing, wearing clean clothes, combing our hair, etc., which help us look neat and keep us fit—are also good habits. A walk in the morning is a good habit for everyone. Man is a social animal, and he cannot live in isolation. Respecting elders, wishing 'Good morning,' 'Good evening', and 'Good night' are good habits.

Good habits include serving the poor and needy and respecting social laws like observing queues. Education is based on the principle of habit formation. Repetition makes learning easy. Learning a language, such as speaking, reading, and writing, is also based on habit.

Similarly, education helps develop good habits like punctuality, attention, concentration, cooperation, discipline, etc.
Good habits lead to good manners. Good manners give us good friends, and 'good friends' means a good environment. A good environment leads to a happy and peaceful life for all in society and in a nation.

Picture Description of a Magician

(7) Look at the Comic Picture and write a paragraph in about 100 words.

A Magician

There came a magician in our school last week. He was none but our Gafur Mia from the neighboring village. He took a white handkerchief from Ruma. He put it into his long brown cap on a wooden tool. Gili, Gili, Gili… choo-mantar, he made a round his magic stick over the cap, and the white handkerchief turned to be a white cat. Mew, MEOUW!!
Our teacher said, 'Magic is nothing but tricks and science.' Whatever it would be, it was a day of great fun for all students to see the tricks or magic of Gafur Mia on the day.

Traffic Signals

(8) Suppose you were going to your school on a walk along a road, and you saw an accident happen. Now, read the traffic rules carefully in succeeding posters and write down a paragraph on **'Traffic Signals'**, the causes of an accident, and how we can avoid such a tragic occurrence.

Causes: Breaking traffic rules, fast driving, animals on roads, Cyclists moving on the wrong lane.

Safety Rules: Follow traffic light signals, maintain the speed limit, and avoid using music or mobile phones while driving.

How to cross the road

- Hold your mother's or your dad's hand tight.

- Find a safe place to cross.

- Stop at the road sign.

- Think carefully.

- Look left.

- Look right and all around you.

- Listen to the horns of the cars, if any is coming?

- Cross safely and remember these rules.

Accidents are Tragic

____

____

____

____

3. PARAGRAPHS on ANIMALS, BIRDS & INSECTS

A paragraph is a piece of writing that is short in length, consists of a few lines or sentences, and begins and ends only in one section. If the writing (on a particular subject) consists of several paragraphs, it is **an Essay**. For more about the terms, please visit the first chapter, 'Introduction.'

In paragraph or essay writing, we generally follow the following guidelines:

- We carefully read the outlines, clues, or pictures and express them in several complete sentences.
- However, in essay writing, we must do more research to collect more information and arrange and express it in more sentences and paragraphs (at least three for the Introduction, Body, and Conclusion). The body may include more paragraphs as necessary.
- We write a title for both a paragraph and an essay. We develop the points given.
- Sometimes, we need to add more details to the thoughts or outlines given. Then, a paragraph tends to become an essay.

To be noted: We have already written some paragraphs in the previous sections to describe a picture given, which is also called **'Picture Story Composition.'** Here, we will discuss the same things, only using the points, and see how they are developed into paragraphs. **Please Study the examples:**

The Elephant

(1) Write a short paragraph on **'The Elephant'**.

Step 1: Give a Title → The Elephant

Step 2: Make an Outline with topic words: *(if that was not given beforehand; like,)* → a wild animal— tamed by man – found in southern Bharat – its appearance – its food – its uses – the elephants in Bharat.

Step 3: Expanding the outlines or points into Sentences to make a paragraph: →

The Elephant

The elephant is a wild animal. But it can be tamed by man. It is found in large numbers in Kerala and Karnataka. It lives in thick forests there. The elephant is the most giant land animal. It is dark in color. It has a large trunk. It has two tusks of ivory. Its food is simple. It eats grass and leaves. It loves to eat sugarcane and banana plants. The elephant has many uses. It can lift and carry heavy loads. It is also used in religious processions. In ancient times, kings and queens rode elephants, widely used in battles. Elephants have been being used in Bharat for centuries.

Tortoise

(2) **Use the points and write a short paragraph on tortoises. (*They are happy, have a hard shell, walk slowly, and live longer than humans.)***

[In the following, three paragraphs are written using the same points written above, but in three dimensions: the first is about fifty words, the second is about seventy words, and the third is within 90 words to see how points can be expanded with new words and expressions, and they can be made short as necessary.]

Sample 1

Tortoises belong to reptiles. It has hard shells. The hard shell protects it from outward threats. Tortoises can vary in size. Some swim best, others generally walk. They stroll, and they always look happy. A tortoise lives longer than animals around us and even longer than human beings. (50 words)

Sample 2

Tortoises are part of the reptile family and are characterized by their hard shells, which protect them from external threats. These fascinating creatures come in various sizes; some excel at swimming, while others are adept at walking on land. Known for their slow and steady pace, tortoises often exude a sense of contentment as they stroll along. These resilient animals boast a longer lifespan than most other creatures, including humans. (70 words)

Sample 3

Tortoises are fascinating reptiles characterized by their hard shells, which protect them from external threats. These creatures can come in various sizes, and while some species are adept swimmers, others are more inclined to walk on land. Known for their leisurely pace, tortoises are often seen moving slowly, yet they always appear content and at peace with their surroundings. One of the most remarkable aspects of tortoises is their impressive longevity, as they typically outlive many other creatures in their environment and can even surpass the lifespan of human beings. (90 words)

Deer

(3) **Use the points and write a short paragraph on Deer. (*Deer live on grass in the forest and run very fast. They have antlers that many animals do not have.)***

Deer are fascinating mammals closely related to cows, elephants, and humans. They are commonly found in lush green grasslands and dense jungles. A male deer is known as a buck, while a female deer is called a doe. However, larger males are often called stags, and female deer are called hinds. The young ones are called fawns. Known for their remarkable agility, deer can leap up to 10 feet high and are also skilled swimmers. They are adept runners on both grass and land. One of the most striking features of deer is their antlers, a characteristic unique to the species. Antlers are considered the fastest-growing living tissue in the animal kingdom. Each year, antlers shed and regrow, showcasing this incredible natural phenomenon. With over 60 species found worldwide, deer can be observed on every continent except Antarctica. While most species of deer possess antlers, some exceptions, such as the Chinese water deer, exist.

Pet Dog

(4) **Use the points and write a short paragraph on a Pet Dog. *(Pet dogs are different in color and species worldwide and are loyal and faithful animals, among all others.)***

Dogs are known for their unwavering loyalty and faithfulness to their owners. They quickly form strong bonds and become beloved pets in no time. A wide variety of dog species is found across the globe, each exhibiting distinct sizes, colors, and characteristics. Dogs have an exceptional sense of smell, estimated to be at least 40 times more sensitive than humans. Some dog breeds display remarkable swimming abilities and impressive speed on land. Unlike humans, dogs have fewer sweat glands and rely on panting to regulate their body temperature.

Horse

(5) **Use the points and write a short paragraph on Horse. (*horse, four strong legs, beautiful crest upon the neck; many love horse riding.)***

Horses, majestic and powerful creatures, are domesticated animals like cows and goats. These odd-toed and hooved mammals are known for their four strong legs, enabling them to sprint at remarkable speeds. Horses are renowned for their intelligence and can sleep while standing up. Interestingly, a male horse has 40 teeth, whereas a mare, a female horse, has only 36. Furthermore, horses rely solely on nasal breathing and cannot breathe through their mouths like humans. Widely used for riding and transportation, many have cherished horses as pets since ancient times.

Honeybee

(6) **Use the points and write a short paragraph on tortoises. (*Honeybees collect nectar from flowers and store it in a hundred rooms called honeycombs.)***

Honey bees, part of the insect family, are small and easily recognizable by their distinctive yellow and black colors, with wings and a stinger that commands respect. Their natural habitats include grasslands, forests, and gardens, but humans have also started rearing them due to their economic significance. Honey bees collect nectar from flowers, which they use to produce and store honey in numerous beehives. When these beehives are full of honey, they form what we know as a honeycomb. Humans then harvest this honey from the honeycombs, making it a valuable resource with significant economic importance.

Peacock

(7) **Use the points and write a short paragraph on the Peacock. (The peacock is the largest and heaviest bird in India, with a crown on its head and dazzling, colorful feathers. It is the national bird of *India.)***

The peacock, renowned for its captivating beauty, is the largest and heaviest flying bird, although it doesn't soar to great heights. With a small mouth and a majestic body weighing about 5 to 10 kg, the peacock possesses a crown and a long, iridescent dark blue neck. Its stunning feathers display a mesmerizing array of colors. When the peacock gracefully dances in the rain, unfurling and rippling its resplendent feathers, it offers a sight that brings instant comfort and joy to our eyes. Recognized for its magnificent beauty and its significant religious significance in Bharatiya traditions, the peacock holds the esteemed position of the National Bird of Bharat.

Write a short essay on peacock: (How would that be? See the example.)

The peacock, scientifically known as Pavo cristates, is the largest and heaviest member of the pheasant family and is renowned for its stunning plumage. The peacock can fly despite its size, although it tends to fly only short distances and not very high off the ground. The male peacock, known as peafowl, is adorned with vibrant and iridescent feathers that feature striking colors. These colors include shimmering blues, greens, and browns, creating an awe-inspiring display that has captivated human admiration for centuries.

The peacock's mesmerizing tail feathers, or train, are particularly noteworthy. They comprise long, elegant covers that can be fanned out in a dramatic display during courtship rituals. This courtship display, often seen during the monsoon season, involves the male peacock fanning its feathers and dancing to attract a mate. The exquisite beauty of the peacock, mainly when it dances in the rain, is truly a sight to behold.

In addition to its physical beauty, the peacock holds significant cultural and symbolic importance in various traditions. In Bharatiya traditions, the peacock is revered as a symbol of grace, beauty, and spirituality. Due to its cultural significance and striking appearance, the peacock has been honored as the National Bird of Bharat, representing the region's deep-rooted cultural and religious heritage.

4. PARAGRAPH / ESSAY on PERSON, PERSONALITIES

To be noted: It's important to note that an essay typically consists of at least three paragraphs that discuss or describe a specific topic. An essay comprises three main sections: Introduction, Body, and Conclusion, each addressing different aspects of the subject matter. In contrast, paragraph writing combines the Introduction, Body, and Conclusion within a single paragraph, differing mainly in length. An essay contains more words, lines, and paragraphs, whereas a paragraph consists of only one.

When discussing various aspects of an event, object, place, person, or idea, sentences naturally break at certain points. Therefore, it is easy to expand a paragraph into an essay by adding more information, lines, and paragraphs. Equally, an essay can be condensed into a paragraph by removing unnecessary information, lines, and paragraphs.

Descriptive writing is suited to writing paragraphs or essays on persons, places, animals, birds, insects, etc. while writing paragraphs or essays on things, events, situations, experiences, or slogans is more Narrative Writing. Study the following:

My Best Friend

(8) **Write a descriptive writing about your Best Friend:**

Fundamentals: The following pointers or clues should be remembered for your paragraph:
Name, Age, size, and other Qualities (like his likes and dislikes). You may also point out some **things in common** between you and your friend.

You may begin like this:

We are both in class one.
We both like to watch cartoon shows, etc.

Study the following model:

Title

My Best Friend

- My best friend name is Rita Thakur.
- She is six years old.
- She is tall and smart. → Size
- We study in the same school.
- She sits next to me in class.
- She is very pretty. → Describing words
- Her favourite cartoon show is Tom and Jerry.
- She likes eating strawberries.
- She likes to play badminton. → Likes
- Her favourite subject is English.
- I like her very much.

❖ **However, you may answer these questions to get clues or information about your best friend.**

a) Name: ______________________________ Age: ________
b) How do you know him/her? ___________________________
c) What does your best friend look like? (Use describing words to describe him/her?)______________

Some questions you may also ask to know his likes and dislikes like:

d) What is her favorite cartoon show? = ______________________
e) What is her favorite fruit? = ______________________
f) What game does she like to play? = ______________________
g) What is her favorite color? =______________________
h) What subjects does she enjoy the most? = __________________________

❖ **The answers to the above questions will guide you in forming a paragraph about your best friend.**

Title ____________________________________

____
____
____
____
____

Another Example: Suppose one of your friends is Raman, who is very gentle and polite to you. You regard him as your best friend. Describe him in 100 words.

Try answering these questions: his name—how or where did you meet—how is he a person- or mention his characteristics—does he help you? How? —affection between you—any incident to recall about your friend. Write a title for your paragraph. Try to give an introduction and a conclusion.

Raman is my best friend

I have several friends, but Raman is my best friend. We are classmates; he has always been there for me during tough times. He is also a constructive critic, which helps me improve. As a top student, he often helps me with my studies. We frequently do homework together and hang out in the evenings. Sometimes, we attend parties or take short trips. I enjoy his company and have learned a lot from him. He is a great mentor and a wise philosopher. In conclusion, he has been a great blessing to me, and I hope our friendship lasts forever. (103 words)

(9) **Write a paragraph about your 'parent' and explain why you like him or her.**

My Father, My Hero

My father is my mentor, my hero, and my best friend. He has always supported me and taught me invaluable life lessons. He believed in leading a simple life and instilled moral values in us. His teachings guide me, and I am proud to follow in his footsteps. I would express my love and gratitude to him if he were alive today. (64 words)

Sample 2

My Father, My Hero

The most influential figure in my life is undeniably my father. He has been my guiding light, strength source, and dearest friend. Throughout my life, his unwavering support and invaluable life lessons have shaped me into the person I am today. His commitment to living a simple life and his dedication to instilling strong moral values in us have profoundly impacted me. I continue to be guided by his teachings and take great pride in walking the same path he once did. If he were here with me today, I would express my boundless love and endless gratitude to him. (110 words)

(10) **Let's write a few sentences about a great man 'Rabindra Nath Tagore.'** **(points:** famous Bharatiya Bengali writer, poet, singer, etc. Geetanjali won him the Noble Prize in 1913—he composed the national anthems of Bharat and Bangladesh—born on 7 May 1861 and died on 7 August 1941.**)**

Rabindra Nath Tagore

One of the most famous Bengali writers in India was Rabindranath Tagore. He was a poet, singer, painter, playwright, composer, philosopher, social reformer, and writer. His work "Gitanjali," a collection of poems and songs, earned him the prestigious Nobel Prize in 1913. The book was first published in 1911 in Bengali and later translated into English in 1912. Rabindranath Tagore also composed "Amar Shonar Bangla," the national anthem of Bangladesh, and "Jana Gana Mana," the national anthem of India. In addition to these compositions, he wrote numerous patriotic folk songs, thousands of other songs and poems, and over a hundred short stories, novels, and essays. This great poet was born on May 7, 1861, in Jorasanko, Thakurbari, Kolkata, and died at eighty on August 7, 1941.

(11) **Describe your favorite dancer, Madhuri Dixit.**
Answer these questions: (who is he or she? (Introducing the man)—what are his or her skills? What performance did you like most?—what's the specialty? (Any *award or honor (national, international) —concluding line).* Give a title to your paragraph.

[**Also can be written:** a paragraph on a dance performance you saw recently.']

Madhuri Dixit is My Favorite Dancer

I have encountered many dancers and am a dancer and performer, but Madhuri Dixit is my favorite. She is an Indian actress and a classical dancer who has received praise from critics for her dancing skills. Once, when I visited Chennai, I was fortunate enough to get four tickets to attend a dance show. To my delight, Madhuri Dixit was performing in the show, and I had the opportunity to witness her excellent dancing and acting skills. As soon as she began to dance, the audience stood up, clapped, and cheered in appreciation. Her movements were captivating, and she communicated beautifully through her dance postures. It felt as though dance was a natural part of her being. While she danced as a whole, upon closer observation, it was evident that every part of her body was dancing individually. In 2008, the Government of India honored her with the Padma Shri award. She has also received numerous other accolades at film festivals for her outstanding dancing and acting. I aspire to become a classical dancer like her. Dance and music have the power to eliminate our boredom within seconds and refresh our bodies and souls. Long live art and culture.

(12) **Write a paragraph on the famous music composer and singer A.R. Rahman.**

Here are the traits of a musician. Use these to write a short biography of about 100 -150 words. You may collect more information from the Internet, books in the library, and other sources.

(A. R. Rahman: Bharatiya composer, singer, songwriter, music producer, musician and philanthropist; born.in Chennai on 6 January 1967; graduated from Trinity College, Oxford University; famous for integrating Bharatiya classical music with electronic music, world music, and traditional orchestral arrangements; recipient of the Padma Shri and the Padma Vibhushan awards; two Oscars and a Golden Globe; a notable humanitarian and philanthropist; donates and raises money for several causes and charities.)

A.R. Rahman, the famous music composer & singer

A.R. Rahman (Allah Rakha Rahman) is an Indian composer, singer, songwriter, music producer, musician, and philanthropist. He was born in Chennai on 6 January 1967 and was known as A.S. Dileep Kumar before converting from Hinduism to Islam. Rahman graduated from Trinity College, Oxford University. He is often referred to as 'the Mozart of Madras' due to his extensive work for film and stage. Rahman made his debut with the movie 'Roja.' He is renowned for blending Indian classical music with electronic music, world music, and traditional orchestral arrangements. Rahman has been honored with the Padma Shri and the Padma Vibhushan awards, and he has won two Oscars and a Golden Globe. In addition to his musical accomplishments, he is a notable humanitarian and philanthropist involved in various charity works, donating and raising money for different causes and charities. I wish this great man a long and prosperous life.

(13) **Based on the following inputs, write a short descriptive Essay on the famous Bharatiya scientist Sir CV Raman.**

(Sir Chandrasekhar Venkat Raman, a great Indian Scientist, Born on 7 November 1888 in Madras—Physician by profession—worked in the field of light scattering—the discovery is known as the 'Raman Effect'—won Nobel Prize in 1930 for his discovery—elected as 'Fellow of the Royal Society' in 1924—in 1954 Bharat honored him with its highest civilian award 'Bharat Ratna' in 1954 —breathed his last on 21 November 1970.)

C.V. Raman, the famous Bharatiya Scientist

Sir Chandrasekhar Venkat Raman, a renowned Indian physicist and Nobel laureate, was born November 7, 1888, in Madras, India. He initially pursued a career in medicine but transitioned to the field of physics, where he made groundbreaking contributions to the study of light scattering, famously known as the 'Raman Effect.' His pioneering work led to discovering the phenomenon where light changes its wavelength when passing through a transparent material. This discovery earned him the Nobel Prize in Physics in 1930, making him the first Asian and non-white person to receive this honor in the field of science.

In addition to this esteemed recognition, Raman was elected as a 'Fellow of the Royal Society' in 1924, further highlighting his influential role in the scientific community. His exceptional contributions and dedication to scientific research were acknowledged by

his home country, as he was posthumously awarded the highest civilian honor, the 'Bharat Ratna,' in 1954.
Chandrasekhar Venkat Raman's legacy continues to inspire and impact the field of physics. He is remembered as one of the most influential scientists of the 20th century. He passed away on November 21, 1970, leaving a remarkable and enduring scientific legacy.

(14) **Study the following points and develop them into a descriptive Essay.**

- *Name:* Dr. Kiran Mazumdar Shaw, a Bharatiya billionaire entrepreneur
- *Parents:* Gujarati; Father Rasendra Mazumdar, formerly head brewmaster at United Breweries.
- *Inspiration:* Father Mazumdar suggested she study fermentation science.
- *Education:* Schooling from Bishop's Cotton Girls' High School, Bachelor's degree in Zoology from Bangalore University, Went to Melbourne University (Australia) to study Malting and Brewing (1974), earned as a master brewer in 1975.
- *Position or rank:* Chairperson and Managing Director at Biocon Limited and Biocon Biologics, a biotechnology company in Bangalore
- *Most Memorable event:* February 2014; First woman to head the board of governors of the Bharatiya Institute of Management Bangalore (IIMB)
- *Other Recognition:* Honored with numerous national and international awards

Dr. Kiran Mazumdar Shaw, a Bharatiya billionaire entrepreneur

Kiran Mazumdar Shaw is an influential Indian entrepreneur and the visionary leader behind Biocon Limited and Biocon Biologics Limited, eminent biotechnology companies headquartered in Bangalore. Born on March 23, 1953, in Bangalore, Karnataka, she began her educational journey at Bishop Cotton Girl's High School before pursuing a bachelor's degree in zoology at Bangalore University. Her thirst for knowledge and innovation led her to Melbourne University in Australia, where she studied malting and brewing, inspired by her father. Standing out as the only woman in her brewing course, she achieved remarkable success, earning the prestigious title of master brewer in 1975.

Returning to India after her time as a trainee brewer at Carlton and United Breweries in Melbourne, Kiran exhibited her entrepreneurial spirit by founding Biocon India in 1978, initiating the company from the confines of her rented house's garage in Bengaluru with a humble seed capital of just Rs. 10,000. This marked the birth of a transformative journey as Biocon evolved into a prominent entity under her astute leadership.

Continuing her pursuit of pioneering advancements, in 1984, Kiran spearheaded the development of a robust research and development team at Biocon, emphasizing the exploration of novel enzymes and the innovation of cutting-edge techniques for solid substrate fermentation technology. This strategic move propelled Biocon to the forefront of biotechnology innovation, solidifying its position as an industry leader. In 1989, Biocon became the first Indian biotech company to receive U.S. funding for proprietary technologies. Kiran Mazumdar Shaw effectively utilized the funds she received, and within a few years, her business took off.

In February 2014, Kiran Mazumdar-Shaw became the first woman to head the board of governors of the Bharatiya Institute of Management Bangalore (IIMB). She has been honored with national and international awards, including the Othmer Gold Medal (2014), and she was elected as a member of the United States National Academy of Engineering (NAE) in 2019. In January 2020, she became the fourth Bharatiya citizen to be honored with Australia's highest civilian honor. She has also received national awards, including the Padma Shri (1989) and the Padma Bhushan (2005), for her contributions to the biotechnology sector.

(15) **Write a biography of Maulana Abul Kalam Azad** (within 100-150 words) based on the following inputs.
(Born on 11 November 1888—composed poetry in Urdu—worked as a journalist, protested against British Raj—an enthusiastic supporter of Gandhiji's ideas—wrote many books, like 'India Wins Freedom,' Ghubar-e-khatir' etc.—first education minister of Independent Bharat—birthday celebrated as National Education Day—died on 22 February 1958.)

Maulana Abul Kalam Azad, Indian Independence Activist

Maulana Abul Kalam Azad, also known as Abul Kalam Ghulam Muhiyuddin Ahmed bin Khairuddin Al-Hussaini Azad, was an Indian independence activist, Islamic theologian, writer, and a senior leader of the Indian National Congress. He was born on 11th November 1888. Azad worked as a journalist and protested against the British Raj through his articles and published news supporting the Indian Freedom Movement. He was an enthusiastic supporter of Gandhi's ideas. He also composed poetry in Urdu and wrote many books, such as 'India Wins Freedom' and 'Ghubar-e-Khatir.' After India gained independence, he became the first Education Minister of Independent India. Soon after, Azad became known as Maulana Azad among the Indian people. In recognition of his role in laying the foundation of education in India, Maulana Azad's birthday is celebrated as National Education Day in India. He passed away on 22nd February 1958.

(16) **Write an essay on**

A.P.J. Abdul Kalam, the Missile Man of India

Dr. A.P.J. Abdul Kalam, also known as the Missile Man of India, significantly contributed to the development of ballistic missiles in India. Born in Rameswaram, Tamil Nadu, in 1931 to Jainulabudeen and Ashiamma, he hailed from a humble Tamil Muslim family and began supporting them financially from a young age. Kalam graduated from St Joseph's College, Tiruchirappalli, in 1954 and completed his studies in aerospace engineering at the Madras Institute of Technology, Chennai, in 1960.

His career included stints at organizations such as the Defense Research and Development Organization (DRDO) and the Indian Space Research Organization (ISRO). He was the project director of India's first indigenous Satellite Launch Vehicle (SLV-III). Kalam played a crucial role in the successful Pokhran-II nuclear tests of 1998 and received several prestigious awards, including the Bharat Ratna, Padma Bhushan, and Padma Vibhushan.

Apart from his scientific achievements, Kalam was also a prolific writer and author of several books, including "Wings of Fire," "Ignited Minds," "Target 3 Billion," "Turning Points," "India 2020," and "My Journey." Known for his love for children, he often interacted with and motivated them, especially during his tenure as the President of India.

(17) **Write an essay on**

Mahatma Gandhi, the Father of the Nation

Mahatma Gandhi was a great freedom fighter who dedicated his life to fighting for the independence of India. He was born into a Hindu family on October 2, 1869, in Porbandar, Gujarat. Throughout his life, he led the Indian people, and his story continues to inspire us. In his battle against British rule, he employed non-violence and the Satyagraha Movement to attain freedom. Despite being arrested and imprisoned numerous times, his unwavering spirit, bravery, and love for the country kept him going, rallying the nation toward liberation from British rule.

His influence extended nationwide, and his principles of 'Non-violence' and 'Satyagraha Movement' were instrumental in compelling the British to retreat from India on August 15, 1947. Since then, August 15 has been celebrated annually as Independence Day in India.

Tragically, after India gained independence, Mahatma Gandhi was assassinated by Nathuram Godse on January 30, 1948. Some individuals, even today, venerate Godse, which is ironic considering his heinous act. May God rest the great soul after completing his noble deeds on this earth.

Gandhiji illuminated our lives by demonstrating that everything is achievable through nonviolence and unity. He is rightfully honored as the father of the nation and continues to live on in the hearts of every Indian citizen. We pay our respects and fondly remember him as the “Father of the Nation.”

Write a short paragraph in about sixty words on Mahatma Gandhi:

Mahatma Gandhi was a revered freedom fighter who led India to independence through non-violence and the Satyagraha Movement. His efforts led to India gaining independence from British rule on August 15, 1947. Tragically, he was assassinated on January 30, 1948. He is fondly remembered as the "Father of the Nation" and continues to inspire people with his principles of non-violence and unity.

(18) **Write an essay on**

Mother Teresa, Saint Teresa of Kolkata

Mother Teresa was a very religious and famous woman and is widely regarded as one of the most outstanding personalities in the world. She dedicated her life to serving as a mother figure, providing kind and selfless service to society's needy and poor people. She is also known as “Saint Teresa of Calcutta,” “angel,” or “a beacon in the world of darkness” to people around the world.

Mother Teresa was born to a religious Catholic family on August 26, 1910, in Skopje, Macedonia. She was baptized the day after her birth, and the date of her baptism, August 27, is considered by many to be her actual birthday. She was given the birth name Anjezë Gonxhe Bojaxhiu. Mother Teresa became a nun at the age of twelve and later joined a convent in 1928 after her father's death. After living in Skopje, Anjeze moved to Ireland and India, where she spent the rest of her life. Upon arrival in India, she moved to Darjeeling at Loreto Convent to continue her training as a Sister. After training, she moved to Kolkata and started serving the poor and distressed in the slums.

In 1950, Mother Teresa established the 'Missionaries of Charity,' an organization with over 4,500 nuns serving in over 133 countries as of 2012. The organization assists people suffering from various difficulties and manages homes for those dying of HIV/AIDS, leprosy, and tuberculosis. Additionally, it operates soup kitchens, dispensaries, mobile clinics, children's and family counseling programs, orphanages, and schools. Members of the organization take vows of chastity, poverty, obedience, and a fourth vow to provide "wholehearted free service to the poorest of the poor."

Mother Teresa wore a simple white sari with a blue border and was revered as a great soul and saint. Her life and work continue to inspire respect and love from people worldwide.

(19) **Write a biography of Annie Besant based on the following hints:**
[***Hints:*** *born 1st October 1847 in London—famous British writer—well-known socialist, activist for the rights of women—participated in Bharatiya politics—joined the Bharatiya National Congress—became the first woman President of the Bharatiya National Congress in 1917—passed away on 20th September 1933 in Madras, Bharat.*]

Annie Besant, Women's Rights Activist

Annie Besant was a British socialist, educationalist, and women's rights activist known for her role in fostering the Home Rule Movement in Bharat. As an educationalist, she has contributed to the organization as one of the founders of Banaras Hindu University. This British writer, socialist, and educationalist was born on 1st October 1847 in London. Besides being a famous writer and activist for women's rights, Annie Besant played an important role in the Independent Movement of Bharat. She actively became involved in Bharatiya politics and joined the Bharatiya National Congress. When World War I broke out in 1914, she helped launch the Home Rule League campaign for democracy in Bharat and the dominion status within the British Empire. This led to her election as the first woman president of the Bharatiya National Congress in late 1917. After the war, she continued the campaign for Bharatiya Independence, and in 1933, this great soul left us forever, leaving her permanent impression in the hearts of all Bharatiyas.

Childhood of Rabindra Nath Tagore

(20) Write eight sentences about Rabindranath Tagore's childhood. Here are some points to help you write the paragraph.
(**hints:** born on 8th May 1861—did not enjoy formal schooling—was taught at home—mathematics teacher was Aghore Babu—used to play in the veranda—role-played as a teacher—taught the railing bars as if they were students—conclusion).

'How Little Rabi Was'

The great poet Rabindranath Tagore was just like us in his boyhood and childhood days and also different from us in some aspects. He was born on 8th May 1861 at Jorasanko, Thakur Bari, Kolkata. Unlike us, Rabindranath did not enjoy formal schooling. He was taught at home with teachers assigned to him. Little Rabi was much influenced by the manners and techniques of his Aghore Sir, the mathematics teacher. In his absence, Little Rabi often acted his role. He used to play in the long and wide verandah of their house and acted as his teacher, Aghore Sir. He taught the railing bars as if they were his students. Like us, little Rabi liked to play and act like an elder, but he could not enjoy formal education like we do, such as going to school and playing in the playground with others. Little Rabi later became the famous Rabindranath Tagore, who won one of the most prestigious awards, the Nobel Prize in Literature.

Henry Louis Vivian Derozio

(21) Use the following hints and write ten sentences about Henry Louis Vivian Derozio: (**Date of Birth & Place:** 18 April 1809, Entally, Kolkata; **Parents:** Francis Derozio & Sophie Johnson; **Education:** 'David Drummond's Dhurramtala Academy,' Presidency College & University; **Profession:** Teacher of English Literature and History at Hindu College; **Achievements:** served as Assistant Editors of 'The Bharat Gazette,' 'The Calcutta Gazette,' 'The East Indian' & 'The Bengal Annual,' etc. **Notable works / Books:** 'To India, My Native Land,' 'The Harp of India,' 'The Fakir of Jungheera,' etc. **Died** on **26 December 1831 in** Kolkata.)

Henry Louis Vivian Derozio

A Bharatiya poet, writer, teacher, and philosopher, Henry Louis Vivian Derozio was primarily notable for his radical ideas and the Young Bengal Movement in Bengal's first half of the 19th century. The great personality was born on 18th April 1809 at Entally, Kolkata, to a couple, Francis Derozio and Sophie Johnson, who were Christians by their religion but were Bharatiyas by heart and love. Derozio attended David Drummond's Dhurramtala Academy, Kolkata, for his secondary education. Then, he went to the Presidency College and University for higher education. After completing his studies, Derozio joined the Hindu college as an English Literature and History Assistant Professor. Derozio actively encouraged his pupils to question all authority. His students attacked tradition and custom, demanded education for women, and campaigned for the freedom of thought and expression. The intellectual revolution that Derozio onset (started) among his students in Bengal is known as the 'Young Bengal Movement,' and his followers are known as the 'Derozians.'

Besides being a teacher, Derozio also served as the assistant editor of several newspapers and magazines, like, 'The India Gazette,' 'The Calcutta Gazette 'East India 'The Bengal Annual,' etc. Derozio was also an excellent poet and a good writer. His notable works include 'To Bharat, My Native Land,' 'The Harp of Bharat,' 'The Fakir of Jungheera,' etc. The great poet and teacher died an immature death of cholera on date of 26th December 1831 in Kolkata.

P. V. Sindhu, a famous Sportsperson

(22) Write a few sentences about a famous sportsperson who had brought glory to our country. Use the following heads:

(**hints:** name of the player—place from where he or she comes—childhood days—events in which she or he took part—achievements—conclusion.)

P. V. Sindhu, a Bharatiya badminton Player

Pusarla Venkata Sindhu, shortly P. V. Sindhu, who is considered one of Bharat's most successful sportspersons, is a Bharatiya badminton player who brought glory to our country by winning a long list of medals at the International level, including the last two Olympics of 2016 and 2020.
P. V. Sindhu, the badminton player from Hyderabad, Andhra Pradesh (now in Telangana), was born on 5th July 1995 to the parents of P. V. Ramana & P. Vijaya, who were both former professional volleyball players, played at national and International levels, especially her father. Sindhu lives in Hyderabad with her family and was educated at Auxilium High School and St. Ann's College for Women, Hyderabad, Telangana, Bharat.
Sindhu started playing badminton at eight and joined Pullela Gopichand's Gopichand Badminton Academy. Her career began when she entered the international circuit at the young age of only 14 in 2009. Sindhu has won 419 national and International singles and doubles medals, including two (one silver and a bronze) in the last two Olympics of 2016 and 2020. In 2021, P.V. Sindhu was awarded the Padma Bhushan, the third-highest civilian award in the Republic of Bharat.

Bankim Chandra Chatterjee, a Bengali Novelist

(23) **Bankim Chandra Chatterjee:**

- Bankim Chandra Chatterjee, A prominent Bharatiya cum Bengali novelist, poet, essayist, and journalist of the late 19th century.
- Served as a Deputy Magistrate and Deputy Collector under the British Government and received the 'Rai Bahadur' title in 1891.
- Wrote fourteen high-quality novels popularly known as 'Sahitya Samrat' (Emperor of Literature) in Bengali.
- Author of Bengali novels 'Durgeshnandini(1865)', 'Kapalkundala(1866)', 'Bishbriksha(1873)', 'Anandamath'(1882), 'Devi Choudhurani(1884)'etc.
- Composer of the most famous slogan, **Vande Mataram** ('from Anandamath), personifying Bharat as a Mother Goddess.

Using the above points, write a paragraph on Bankim Chandra Chatterjee in about 100 words.

Bankim Chandra Chattopadhyay

Bankim Chandra Chatterjee was a renowned Indian and Bengali novelist, poet, essayist, and journalist who lived during the late 19th century. He held significant positions as a Deputy Magistrate and Deputy Collector under the British Government and was honored with the 'Rai Bahadur' title in 1891. B.C. Chatterjee is celebrated for his literary contributions and is often called 'Sahitya Samrat' (Emperor of Literature) in the Bengali language. He is the author of a total of fourteen high-quality novels, some of the most famous being 'Durgeshnandini' (1865), 'Kapalkundala' (1866), 'Bishbriksha' (1873), 'Anandamath' (1882), 'Devi Choudhurani' (1884), and others. Notably, he composed the famous slogan "Vande Mataram" (from Anandamath), which reveres India as a Mother Goddess.

Using the above points, write a short essay on Bankim Chandra Chatterjee in about 160 words.

Bankim Chandra Chattopadhyay

One of the prominent figures in Indian and Bengali literature during the late 19th century was Bankim Chandra Chatterjee. He had multifaced talents. He excelled as a novelist, poet, essayist, and journalist and held positions as a Deputy Magistrate and Deputy Collector under the British Government. In recognition of his contributions and achievements, he was granted the prestigious "Rai Bahadur" title in 1891.

His literary prowess shone through in his fourteen high-quality novels, earning him the revered moniker of "Sahitya Samrat" (Emperor of Literature) in Bengali literary circles. Among his notable works are the Bengali novels "Durgeshnandini" (1865), "Kapalkundala" (1866), "Bishbriksha" (1873), "Anandamath" (1882), and "Devi Choudhurani" (1884), all of which left an indelible mark in the realm of Bengali literature.

His impact extended beyond the realm of literature. He also composed the widely famous slogan "Vande Mataram," initially found in the novel 'Anandamath.' This slogan reverentially personifies Bharat (India) as a Mother Goddess, embodying a profound patriotism and love for the nation.

Bibhutibhusan Bandyopadhyay, a Rich Literary Legacy

(24) **Bibhutibhusan Bandyopadhyay**

- Bibhutibhusan Bandyopadhyay, Date of Birth & Place: 12th September, 1894, near at Kalyani, Nadia, W.B.
- Parents: Father Mahananda Bandyopadhyay and mother Mrinalini Devi.
- Early & Higher education: Bangaon High School—Intermediate and graduation from Ripon College, now Surendranath College of Kolkata.
- Profession: worked as Headmaster at Jangipara High School and Harinavi Anglo-Sanskrit Institution.
- Works or Contribution: Famous novels include Pather Panchali, Aparajita, Aranyak, Debjan, Icchamati, and Chander Pahar.
- Died on 1st November 1950, leaving a rich legacy in Bengali literature.

Bibhutibhusan Bandyopadhyay was born on September 12, 1894, near Kalyani in the Nadia district of West Bengal. His parents were Mahananda Bandyopadhyay and Mrinalini Devi. He received his early education at Bangaon High School, completed his intermediate education, and graduated from Ripon College, which is now known as Surendranath College in Kolkata.

Professionally, Bandyopadhyay worked as the headmaster at Jangipara High School and Harinavi Anglo-Sanskrit Institution. He was a dedicated educator and made significant contributions to the field of education.

Bandyopadhyay is best known for his literary works, particularly his famous novels such as "Pather Panchali," "Aparajita," "Aranyak," "Debjan," "Icchamati," and "Chander Pahar," among others. His writing has left an indelible mark on Bengali literature and continues to be celebrated for its timeless appeal.

Tragically, Bibhutibhusan Bandyopadhyay passed away on 1st November 1950, but his literary legacy lives on, captivating readers and inspiring generations to come.

Ishwar Chandra Vidyasagar, the Social Reformer

(25) Ishwar Chandra Bandyopadhyay

- A Bharatiya educator and social reformer of the 19th century, he was popularly known as Ishwar Chandra Vidyasagar for his immense knowledge (in Bengali and Sanskrit) and 'Dayarsagar' for his benevolence and work for the poor and helpless in Bengal.
- **Date of Birth & Place:** 26th September, 1820, at Birsingha village, Purba Midnapore, West Bengal.
- **Parents:** Thakurdas Bandyopadhyay and Bhagvati Devi
- **Education:** at village Pathsala and Kolkata
- **Profession:** joined as a professor in Fort William College, and later in Sanskrit College and University (1829–1841),
- **Works and Contribution:** Simplified and modernized Bengali prose; introduced punctuation marks in Bengali and wrote 'Barna Parichay.' The most prominent campaigner for Hindu widow remarriage, resulting in the ***'Hindu Widows' Remarriage Act, 1856'.*** Established girls' schools and night schools for adults. Fought for tribal & women's rights and education.
- **Died** on: 29th July 1891.

Ishwar Chandra Bandyopadhyay, renowned as Ishwar Chandra Vidyasagar, was a distinguished Indian educator and social reformer whose impact was felt throughout the 19th century. He was affectionately referred to as 'Dayarsagar' due to his compassion and tireless efforts in aiding the impoverished and helpless in Bengal.

Ishwar Chandra was born on September 26, 1820, in Birsingha, Purba Medinipur, West Bengal. He was the son of Thakurdas Bandyopadhyay and Bhagvati Devi. He received his education at the village Pathshala and later in Kolkata.

Ishwar Chandra started his professional journey as a professor at Fort William College, subsequently teaching at Sanskrit College and University from 1829 to 1841. A pioneer in literature, he endeavored to simplify and modernize Bengali prose and introduced punctuation marks in the Bengali language. He authored Barna Parichay, leaving a lasting mark on Bengali literature.

Notably, Ishwar Chandra Vidyasagar was at the forefront of the movement for Hindu widow remarriage. His relentless advocacy resulted in the enactment of the Hindu Widows' Remarriage Act in 1856. Additionally, he established schools for girls and night schools for adults, demonstrating his commitment to education as a tool for social change.

Ishwar Chandra Vidyasagar also championed the rights and education of tribal communities and women. His vision and efforts had far-reaching impacts in shaping a more equitable society.

Ishwar Chandra Vidyasagar passed away on July 29, 1891, leaving a legacy of compassion, social reform, and educational advancement that inspires generations.

Kalpana Chawla, the First Bharatiya Woman Astronaut

(26) **Kalpana Chawla**

- She is the first woman astronaut of Bharatiya's origin to go to space twice: first, in November-December 1997, and then again in January-February 2003, on the NASA space shuttle Columbia.
- **Date of Birth & Place:** 1962, Karnal, Haryana, Bharat.
- **Education:** Aeronautical Engineering from Punjab Engineering College, Bharat, and University of Texas at Arlington, America— Joined as a Research Scientist at NASA Ames Research Centre in Sunnyvale, California, USA.
- **Contribution:** First woman of Bharatiya origin to go to Space and twice. First on Nov-Dec., 1997 (19th Nov-4th Dec. 1997) as a mission specialist and primary robotic arm operator; and January-Feb. 2003 on NASA space shuttle Columbia (16th January to 1st Feb., 2003).

Kalpana Chawla, the trailblazing astronaut of Indian origin, achieved the remarkable feat of venturing into space not once but twice. Her groundbreaking journeys took place first in November-December 1997 and again in January-February 2003 aboard the NASA space shuttle Columbia.

Born in 1962 in Karnal, Haryana, India, Kalpana Chawla possessed an impressive educational background. She pursued Aeronautical Engineering at Punjab Engineering College in India and the University of Texas at Arlington in the United States. She went on to join the esteemed NASA Ames Research Center in Sunnyvale, California, as a Research Scientist.

Kalpana's distinguished contributions to space exploration are truly commendable. She became the first woman of Indian origin to venture into space, achieving this milestone not just once but twice. During her first mission, from November to December 1997, she served as a mission specialist and primary robotic arm operator. Her second NASA space shuttle Columbia mission occurred from January 16th to February 1st, 2003.

Kazi Nazrul Islam, the Rebel Poet

(27) **Kazi Nazrul Islam**

- A soldier, famous Bharatiya Bengali writer, freedom fighter, poet, singer, and playwright who is also popularly known as 'Bidrohi Kobi' or the rebel poet, was born on 24 May 1899 at Churulia near Asansol in the district of Bardhhaman (Burdwan).
- **Parents:** Kazi Faqeer Ahmed, the imam and caretaker of the local Pirpukur mosque and mausoleum of Haji Pahlawan, and Nazrul's mother was Zahida Khatun, a housewife.
- **Schooling or Education:** studied at a maktab and madrasa, run by a mosque and a dargah, respectively, where he studied the Quran, Hadith, Islamic philosophy, and theology. In 1910, Nazrul took enrollment at the Searsole Raj High School in Raniganj. In school, his teacher, a Jugantar activist, Nibaran Chandra Ghatak, influenced him. He later transferred to the Mathrun High English School. However, I did not appear in the Metriculation Test due to my inability to pay exam fees.

- **Contribution:** founder of **'Nazrul Geeti'** (the folk songs in Bengali) and writer of many patriotic songs like 'Karar oi louha kopat', 'We shall Overcome', 'Bidrohi', etc.
- The great poet moved to Bangladesh in 1972 on the invitation of the government. Four years later, on 29 August 1976, the great poet breathed his last at Dhaka, Bangladesh.

Kazi Nazrul Islam, widely recognized as the rebel poet, was a multifaceted personality - a soldier, a prominent Bengali writer, a freedom fighter, a poet, a singer, and a playwright. He was born on 24th May 1899 in Churulia near Asansol, in the district of Bardhaman (Burdwan). His father, Kazi Faqeer Ahmed, was an imam and caretaker of the local Pirpukur mosque and mausoleum of Haji Pahlawan, while his mother, Zahida Khatun, was a housewife.

During his early education, he studied at a maktab and madrasa, where he studied the Quran, Hadith, Islamic philosophy, and theology. Later, in 1910, Nazrul joined the Searsole Raj High School in Raniganj. His teacher, Nibaran Chandra Ghatak, a Jugantar activist, greatly influenced him. Subsequently, he transferred to the Mathrun High English School. Unfortunately, he could not appear for the Matriculation Test due to financial constraints.

Nazrul Islam was the founder of 'Nazrul Geeti,' a genre of folk songs in Bengali, and authored many patriotic songs such as 'Karar oi louha kopat,' 'We shall Overcome,' and 'Bidrohi.' His contributions to literature and music are a significant part of Bengali cultural heritage.

In 1972, he was invited by the government of Bangladesh, where he spent his final years. On 29th August 1976, Kazi Nazrul Islam passed away in Dhaka, Bangladesh, leaving behind a rich and enduring legacy.

Mary Kom, an Amateur Boxer

(28) Mary Kom

- Mangte Chungneijang Mary Kom (born 24 November 1982) is a Bharatiya **amateur boxer**, politician, and former Member of Parliament, Rajya Sabha.
- **Born:** 24 November 1982, Kangathei, Manipur. Bharat.
- **Medals:** She is the only woman boxer to win the **World Amateur Boxing Championship** six times, the only female boxer to have won a medal in each one of the first **seven World Championships**, and the only boxer (male or female) to win **eight World Championship medals**.

Mangte Chungneijang Mary Kom, also known as Mary Kom, is a prominent figure in Indian sports and politics. Born on November 24, 1982, in Kangathei, Manipur, India, she is a distinguished amateur boxer, a respected politician, and a former Member of Parliament in the Rajya Sabha.

Mary Kom's achievements in boxing are genuinely remarkable. She is the only woman boxer to clinch the World Amateur Boxing Championship title six times. Additionally, she is the sole female boxer to have secured a medal in the first seven World

Championships, highlighting her consistent excellence in the sport. Notably, Mary Kom is the only boxer, regardless of gender, to have earned eight World Championship medals, underlining her exceptional talent and dedication to boxing. These outstanding accomplishments have rightfully established her as an icon in boxing.

Milkha Singh, A Bharatiya Athlete

(29) **Milkha Singh**

- Bharatiya track and field athlete, also known as **"The Flying Sikh."** He is the only athlete to win gold in 400 meters at the Asian and Commonwealth Games. He also won **gold medals** in the **1958** and **1962 Asian Games**.
- **Born:** 20 November 1929, Govindpura, (Now in Pakistan)
- **Died:** 18 June 2021, Chandigarh (Bharat)
- **Books:** The Race of My Life (biography)

Milkha Singh, a renowned track and field athlete from India, was affectionately known as "The Flying Sikh" due to his incredible speed and agility. He achieved a remarkable feat by becoming the only athlete to clinch gold in the 400 meters at both the Asian Games and the Commonwealth Games. Additionally, he secured gold medals in the 1958 and 1962 Asian Games, solidifying his athletic legacy. Singh was born on 20 November 1929 in Govindpura, now in Pakistan. He sadly passed away on 18 June 2021 in Chandigarh, India. Furthermore, he penned his autobiography titled "The Race of My Life," offering readers an intimate look into his extraordinary journey.

P. T. Usha, the Sprint Queen of India

(30) **P. T. Usha**

- Pilavullakandi Thekkeraparambil Usha is a retired Bharatiya track and field athlete.
- **Born:** 27 June 1964 at Kuthali, Kozhikode, Kerala, Bharat.
- **1st National Award:** 1977, in the 100-meter sprint at the age of 13.
- **International Awards:** won 4 Asian gold medals and 7 Silver medals along with others.
- Honored with the Title of the **"Queen of Indian Running track and field."** 'Payyoli Express,' 'The Sprint Queen of India,' etc.

Pilavullakandi Thekkeraparambil Usha, also known as P.T. Usha, is a highly acclaimed and retired track and field athlete from Bharat. She was born on 27 June 1964 in Kuthali, Kozhikode, Kerala, Bharat.

At the age of 13, P.T. Usha earned her first National Award in the 100-metre sprint in 1977. Her impressive international career included winning four Asian gold medals, seven silver medals, and numerous other accolades.

P.T. Usha has been honored with several titles, including "Queen of Bharatiya Running Track and Field," "Payyoli Express," and "The Sprint Queen of Bharat." These titles reflect her status as one of Bharat's most influential and successful athletes.

Raja Ram Mohan Roy, A Social Reformer

(31) **Raja Ram Mohan Roy**

- A Bharatiya social reformer and one of the founders of the **Brahmo Sabha in 1828**, the precursor of the Brahmo Samaj, a social-religious reform movement in the Bharatiya subcontinent. For his knowledge and authority in Bengali literature, Akbar II, the Mughal emperor, gave him the title of Raja.
- **Born:** 22 May 1772, Radhanagar, Khanakul
- **Died:** 27 September 1833, Stapleton, Bristol, United Kingdom

Raja Ram Mohan Roy was a prominent Bharatiya social reformer known for founding the Brahmo Sabha in 1828, which ultimately led to the establishment of the Brahmo Samaj. This religious and social reform movement played a significant role in the Bharatiya subcontinent. For his profound knowledge and authority in Bengali literature, Raja Ram Mohan Roy was honored with the title "Raja" by Akbar II, the Mughal emperor.
Raja Ram Mohan Roy was born on 22nd May 1772 in Radhanagar, Khanakul, and he passed away on 27th September 1833 in Stapleton, Bristol, United Kingdom. He was a prominent figure in the Indian Renaissance and significantly contributed to social and religious reforms in India.

Rakesh Sharma, First Bharatiya Cosmonaut

(32) **Rakesh Sharma**

- A Bharatiya Air Force cadet and cosmonaut. First Bharatiya in space on 3rd April, 1984.
- **Date of Birth & Place:** 1949, Patiala, Punjab.
- **Education:** St. George's Grammar School, Hyderabad & Kendriya Vidyalaya, Tirumalagiri, Hyderabad, Bharat.
- **Contribution / Achivement:** First Bharatiya went to space on 3rd April, 1984 on Soyuz T-11, a Russian Space shuttle. Spent 7 days, 21 hours and 40 minutes, working in the fields of bio-medicine and remote sensing with the Russian crew members.

Rakesh Sharma, an Indian Air Force cadet and cosmonaut, became the first Indian in space on April 3, 1984. Rakesh Sharma was born in 1949 in Patiala, Punjab. He attended St. George's Grammar School in Hyderabad and Kendriya Vidyalaya in Tirumalagiri, Hyderabad, India. Rakesh Sharma's groundbreaking journey to space occurred on the Soyuz T-11, a Russian space shuttle. During this mission, he spent seven days, 21 hours, and 40 minutes conducting bio-medicine and remote sensing experiments alongside his Russian crew members. This historic achievement marked an incredible milestone for India's space exploration efforts.

Sarat Chandra Chattopadhyay, Bengali Novelist

(33) **Sarat Chandra Chattopadhyay**

- A prominent Bengali novelist and short story writer of the early 20th century—author of **'Devdas,' 'Parineeta,' 'Srikanta,' 'Rajlakshmi,' 'Pother Dabi,'** and many others.
- He could not complete his graduation due to his inability to pay the examination fees, but he remains the most popular, translated, and adapted Bharatiya author of all time.
- To date, **fifty films** and more have been made in many Bharatiya languages based upon his novels and stories. The most popular are Devdas, Parineeta, Barodidi, Majhli Didi, Rajlakshimi, 'Srikanta,' and 'Swami,' which won him the Filmfare Award for Best Story in 1978.

Sarat Chandra Chattopadhyay was a highly influential Bengali novelist and short story writer during the early 20th century. He is best known for his literary masterpieces, such as Devdas, Parineeta, Srikanta, Rajlakshmi, and Pother Dabi. Despite facing financial constraints that prevented him from completing his graduation due to his inability to pay examination fees, he remains one of the most popular, translated, and adapted Indian authors.
His works have inspired over fifty films in various Indian languages, reflecting the enduring appeal of his stories. Notable cinematic adaptations of his works include Devdas, Parineeta, Barodidi, Majhli Didi, Rajlakshimi O Srikanta, and Swami, which earned him the prestigious Filmfare Award for Best Story in 1978. Sarat Chandra Chattopadhyay's literary legacy continues to enthrall audiences across generations and remains an integral part of Indian cultural heritage.

Satyajit Ray, the Film-maker

(34) **Satyajit Ray**

- A Bharatiya director, screenwriter, documentary filmmaker, author, essayist, lyricist, magazine editor, illustrator, calligrapher, and composer.
- **Born:** 2 May 1921, Kolkata
- **Parents:** Sukumar Ray, the eminent poet, writer & mother, was Suprabha Ray.
- **Books:** Professor Shonku, Sonar Kella, Badshahi Angti, Stories,
- **Films:** Pather Panchali, Ashani Sanket, Apu Trilogy, Nayak, Goopy Gyne Bagha Byne, Hirak Rajar Deshe, Ghare Baire, etc.
- **Awards:** Bharat Ratna, Dadasaheb Phalke Award.
- **Died:** 23 April 1992, Kolkata

Satyajit Ray was a multi-talented Bengali director, screenwriter, documentary filmmaker, author, essayist, lyricist, magazine editor, illustrator, calligrapher, and composer. He was born on 2nd May 1921 in Kolkata to Sukumar Ray, an eminent poet and writer, and Suprabha Ray. Ray's literary works include "Professor Shonku," "Sonar

Kella," "Badshahi Angti," and numerous short stories. Some of his notable films are "Pather Panchali," "Ashani Sanket," "Apu Trilogy," "Nayak," "Goopy Gyne Bagha Byne," "Hirak Rajar Deshe," and "Ghare Baire."
Ray received numerous awards throughout his career, including the prestigious Bharat Ratna and Dadasaheb Phalke Award for his exceptional contribution to Indian cinema. He passed away on 23rd April 1992 in Kolkata, leaving behind a profound legacy in cinema and literature.

Subhas Chandra Bose, the Nationalist Leader

(35) **Subhas Chandra Bose**

- A Bharatiya nationalist leader, a key figure in the Bharatiya Independence Movement against British rule.
- **D/O/B & Place:** 23rd January 1897 in Cuttack, Orissa, Bharat.
- **Parents:** Janakinath Bose and Prabhavati Devi
- **Schooling/Education:** Cuttak, Presidency College (Kolkata) where he studied in philosophy
- **Contribution/Achievement:** During World War II, in 1943, Subhas escaped from house confinement and reached out to Germany to seek help from Hitler. Moved to Japan through Russia. Took charge of '**Azad Hind Fauz**' from Ras Bihari Bose. Declared war against the British and moved his army through Rangoon. With Japan surrendering, the Azad Hind Fauz retreated and was defeated. Many soldiers were either brutally killed or arrested.
- **D/O/D:** Died in 1945 in a plane crash near Taiwan. Remembered for his indomitable valour, motif and selfless sacrifice for the country. One of our National Heroes and alive in the hearts of all Bharatiyas.

Subhas Chandra Bose was a prominent Bharatiya nationalist leader who played a significant role in the Bharatiya Independence Movement, striving for freedom from British rule. He was born on 23rd January 1897 in Cuttack, Orissa, Bharat, to Janakinath Bose and Prabhavati Devi.
Bose received his education in Cuttack and later attended Presidency College in Kolkata, where he pursued a degree in philosophy. His academic pursuits set the stage for his future contributions to the independence movement.
During World War II, in 1943, Subhas Chandra Bose bravely escaped from house confinement and sought assistance from Germany, even meeting with Adolf Hitler. He then went to Japan via Russia, where he assumed leadership of the Indian National Army (Azad Hind Fauz) after succeeding Ras Bihari Bose. Bose fearlessly declared war against the British and led his army through Rangoon. However, with the surrender of Japan, the Azad Hind Fauz faced defeat, with many soldiers being either cruelly killed or captured.
Tragically, Subhas Chandra Bose's life was cut short when he died in a plane crash near Taiwan in 1945. His legacy lives on as he is remembered for his unwavering courage, dedication, and selfless devotion to the country. Subhas Chandra Bose is revered as one of our national heroes and continues to hold a special place in the hearts of all Bharatiyas.

Sunita Williams, the American Astronaut

(36) **Sunita Williams or Sunita Lyn Williams**

- An American astronaut (earlier worked as a United States Navy officer);
- **Born:** 19 September 1965, Euclid, Ohio, United States.
- **Education:** Florida Institute of Technology (1995), United States Naval Academy (1987), Needham High School (1983),
- **Space missions:** was assigned to the International Space Station as a member of Expedition 14 and Expedition 15 and more by NASA. Williams formerly held the records for most spacewalks by a woman and most spacewalk time for a woman. **Space-time:** 321d 17h 15m.

Sunita Williams, also known as Sunita Lyn Williams, is an accomplished American astronaut serving as a United States Navy officer. She was born on September 19, 1965, in Euclid, Ohio, United States. Williams pursued her education at the Florida Institute of Technology (graduating in 1995), the United States Naval Academy (Class of 1987), and Needham High School (Class of 1983).

In her impressive career, Sunita Williams has been involved in several space missions, including being assigned to the International Space Station by NASA as a member of Expedition 14 and Expedition 15. She has set records for the most spacewalks by a woman and the most spacewalk time for a woman. Throughout her career, she has accumulated an impressive total space-time of 321 days, 17 hours, and 15 minutes.

Swami Vivekananda, the Indian Religious Teacher

(37) **Swami Vivekananda**

- A Hindu Monk, philosopher, author, and religious teacher who believed 'Education is the manifestation of perfection already in men.'
- He was the chief disciple of the Bharatiya mystic Ramkrishna Paramhansa.
- **D/O/B:** 12 January 1863, Kolkata, West Bengal
- **Parents:** Vishwanath Datta and Bhubaneswari Devi.
- **Schooling or Education:** Vidyasagar's Metropolitan Institution and the Presidency College, Calcutta.
- **Contribution:** His revolutionary speech in the 1893 Parliament of the World's Religions, held in Chicago, America, attracted the world's attention to the philosophy of Sanatan Hindu religion about the fraternity, unity, tolerance, and coexistence of all regions (as different rivers flow down to meet at one Ocean; different paths, i.e., religious beliefs) finally meet the same Infinity, i.e., God).
- Founded **Vedanta Society of New York** and **Vedanta Society of Northern California.**
- Later, back to Bharat, on 1st May 1897, Swami Vivekananda founded the 'Ramakrishna **Mission'** at Belur Math, Howrah.
- 12th January, the Birthday of Swamiji, is celebrated as the **National Youth Day** in Bharat.
- **D/O/D:** 4th July 1902 at Belur Math. Howrah, West Bengal, Bharat.

Swami Vivekananda, a revered Hindu figure, was a prominent Hindu monk, philosopher, author, and religious teacher whose teachings inspired millions worldwide. He believed that "Education is the manifestation of perfection already in men," emphasizing the innate potential within individuals.

A notable disciple of the renowned mystic Ramakrishna Paramahansa, Swami Vivekananda was born on January 12, 1863, in Kolkata, West Bengal, to Vishwanath Datta and Bhubaneswari Devi. He received his early education at Vidyasagar's Metropolitan Institution and the Presidency College in Calcutta.

Swami Vivekananda gained international attention through his groundbreaking speech at the 1893 Parliament of the World's Religions in Chicago, America. His address shed light on the profound philosophy of Sanatan Hinduism, emphasizing the ideals of fraternity, unity, tolerance, and coexistence of all religions. He famously compared the convergence of diverse religious beliefs to the meeting of different rivers in the ocean—ultimately leading to the same ultimate reality, symbolized as God.

In addition to his influential speeches and teachings, Swami Vivekananda founded the Vedanta Society of New York and Northern California, contributing to the spread of Vedanta philosophy. Upon returning to India, he established the Ramakrishna Mission at Belur Math, Howrah, on 1 May 1897.

Swami Vivekananda's impact is commemorated annually in India with the celebration of National Youth Day on 12 January, his birth anniversary. His legacy continues to resonate, with his passing on 4 July 1902 at Belur Math, Howrah, West Bengal, leaving an indelible mark on the world.

5. PARAGRAPH / ESSAY WRITING on PLACE

While describing a place, there are some important steps:

- Break the description into 2-3 paragraphs.
- Each paragraph dealing a different aspect of the place.
- It is important to ensure continuity in paragraphs.
- If the description has to be written in one paragraph, then include all the details briefly.

(38) You went to your friend's village during your summer vacation. His grandmother looked after you as if you were her grandchild. **Describe this experience in 100-150 words.**

Visiting My Friend's Village Last Summer

During every summer vacation, I usually visit a hill station or a beach. I visited my friend's village, where she lived with her grandparents. She warmly welcomed me, which immediately made me feel at home. On my first day there, I bathed in the nearby river and spent hours wandering in the dense forest. In the evening, her grandmother shared stories with us. Her sweet and soft-spoken nature impressed me and reminded me of my late grandmother. It felt like my grandmother was with us, and at times, I was confused about where I was!

The breakfast, lunch, and dinner her grandmother prepared were tasty and full of love. She cared for all my needs, making me feel like I was in a grandmother's paradise. She also shared many photographs from her album and revealed that she was a champion in swimming, having won numerous gold medals in competitions during her younger days. Seeing her excitement as she shared her experiences made visiting my friend's village enjoyable.

(39) **You visited Darjeeling, a Hill Station in West Bengal, and collected details about it. Based on the following inputs, write a descriptive paragraph of** *100-150 words.*

Fact File

- **Nearest Airport:** Bag Dogra, 69 km. far from Darjeeling.
- **Nearest Railway Station:** Darjeeling Railway Station (only 1.4 km.), famous for its heritage Troy Train, connected with NJP Junction.
- **Main Attractions:** Natural beauty in abundance. Besides, Tenzing Rock, Japanese Buddhist temple, Mahakal Temple, Peace Pagoda, and many more.
- **Best Time to Travel:** October to December
- **Things to Do:**
  → To Experience the jolly toy train ride
  → Shopping tea, etc.
- **Places To Stay:** Sanderling Residency & Spa, Summit Swiss Heritage Hotel & Spa, Summit Hermon Hotel & Spa, Ramada, Green Tara Residency, etc.
- **Ideal Duration to visit main attractions:** at least 2-3 days.

My Visit to Darjeeling, a Hill Station in West Bengal

People from different parts of the world come to experience the exquisiteness in Darjeeling. Darjeeling is one of the most happening hill stations which is at very close distance from Siliguri Town in West Bengal, Bharat. Residing at Darjeeling, one can also visit its nearest attractions like **Tenzing Rock, Japanese Buddhist temple, Mahakal Temple,** and **Peace Pagoda**, and many more when you are in Darjeeling.

The ideal time to visit Darjeeling is between October to December. However, the hotels and lodges here are always ready to welcome. To reach the place by air, Bag Dogra is the nearest airport, about 69 K.M. away from Darjeeling, and road transport is available. Other important tourist attractions include a Jolly Toy train ride and shopping for teas of different flavors near different tea gardens.

Places to Stay: Sanderling Residency & Spa, Summit Swiss Heritage Hotel & Spa, Summit Hermon Hotel & Spa, and Green Tara Residency are a few examples among many other popular resorts in Darjeeling. One can also book online. It will take only three days to visit the main attractions of Darjeeling.

(40) **You recently visited the city of Jaipur, famous for its Hawa Mahal, palace, and forts. Shopping in Jaipur is also exciting,** as there are many things to buy. **Write a description of the place** in 100-150 words.

Visiting Jaipur, a Historical Place

Jaipur is the capital city of Rajasthan. Jaipur is also called the Pink City and is famous for its Hawa Mahal. The Mahal is made of pink stone. The city is colorful with its many monuments, good food, and many historical shopping places. By road from Delhi, it is only about 4 hour' drive. By air, it's only about 45 minutes from Delhi. By weather, Jaipur is hot, and the best time to visit is between December and February. The rest of the months are too hot here for tourists to visit. Like other historical places, the palaces in Jaipur were constructed by erstwhile kings and are marvelous architectural structures. If one has to see all the monuments, it will take no less than three days.

Apart from forts and monuments, Jaipur is also an exciting place for tourists to shop. Things are reasonably priced; marble ***carvings*** and ***objects made out of stone*** are famous in Jaipur. The typical ***Rajasthani cuisine*** (cookery) is elaborate and is served with a lot of butter and ghee. Some of the dishes are ***dal, Bhatti churma, kachori***, etc. The art of **tie and dye** is very famous in Rajasthan. Fabric, dress material, and sarees on which this technique is used are liked by women.

(41) **Srinagar, with its Dal Lake, snow-clad mountain peaks, and Shalimar Garden, is a paradise on** earth. You visited this beautiful city sometime back. **Write an account of the place** in 100-150 words.

Visiting 'Srinagar of Kashmir,' the Paradise on Earth

Kashmir is often called paradise on earth. It is a beautiful, scenic place with snow-clad mountains, beautiful lakes, flowers, and fruits all around. Srinagar, the capital of Kashmir, is connected by air with all major Bharat metros. There is no train facility in Kashmir. The nearest railway station is Katra or Jammu. There are many hotels where one can stay.

In Dal Lake, there are houseboats called Shikaras, where one can also stay. Words cannot describe the beauty of this place. One can see apple trees laden with apples. Other main trees are Deodar, Firs, pines, Chinar, Maple, Birch, and Walnut. One should visit Srinagar at least once during one's lifetime.

(42) **Write a paragraph describing a journey, imaginary, or you have undertaken.** You can follow the steps given below:

1) Prepare an **itinerary** (route of the journey).
2) You can use the following expressions, phrases, and sayings frequently used by travelers.

(Jetlag, itchy feet, hitting the road, timetable, on the home stretch, call it a day, book in advance, travel over, travel through, travel light, any port in a storm, stopover, etc.)

Visiting Thailand

We decided to go to Thailand last month. 'We' means 'me, my parents and my younger sister. I was too excited to think of what it would be like, and it was our first visit abroad. My father booked the tickets, and when the time came, we packed our things. When we landed at Thailand airport after a journey of about five hours, we had jet legs but soon forgot to see the beauty all around the airport. We were thrilled to take our turn to visit the sights. However, we first checked in the hotel and rested for some time. It was a wonderful day, and we enjoyed coconut milk served by the hotel staff. In the afternoon, we hired bikes and toured half of the island, relishing the local life that was so lively and full of activity.

On our way, we tasted the delicacies of the local cuisine. Mostly, it was spicy food. We visited tropical jungles and witnessed the beauty and splendor of nature. We were overwhelmed by the serenity and beauty of the place. And soon, the time arrived to go back. It was a sad moment when you thought of leaving such a place of extraordinary calm so quickly. We spent only three days. Our return tickets were confirmed, and we had to. It was the best journey I took with my parents last month.

(43) **Delhi, the capital of Bharat, is a beautiful amalgamation of tradition and modernity**. With monuments and buildings like the Red Fort, Jama Masjid, India Gate, and Rashtrapati Bhavan, it is a city worth visiting. You happened to go around the town last winter. Write a description of the city in 100-150 words.

Visiting Delhi, a Wonderful City

Delhi, the capital city of Bharat, is a beautiful amalgamation of tradition and modernity. There are many places to visit in this city. It is the most well-connected city in the country. There are various hotels and guest houses where people who visit this city can stay. If one wishes to see all the places in this city, she or he has to stay here for at least 3-4 days. Red Fort, Jama Masjid, Qutub Minar, Bharat Gate, and many other places to visit and see. There are also many shopping malls in Chandni Chowk, Karol Bagh, and Connaught Place. One can feel and see the beautiful blend of the old and the new in the capital city of Bharat.

(44) Suppose you visited Bandhavgarh National Park last December, Madhya Pradesh. **Write a descriptive paragraph on the following inputs** in 100-150 words.

<u>Fact File</u>

- **Place:** Set amongst Vindhya Hills and in the district of Shadol, M.P.
- **Transport facilities/How to reach Destination:**
    - Nearest airport, Jabalpur (165 km)
    - The nearest town and railway head is Umaria (30 km). The other railway stations are Jabalpur (165 km), Katni (102 km) and Satna (120 km).

- **Lodging:** There are varied government and private options for accommodation in Tala village that adjoins the park.
- **Time for Visit:** The park is open from October to June. However, the best season for viewing wildlife is November to April.
- **Getting around:** Maruti Gypsy is used to explore the park. Reservations for the safari can be made at the Project Tiger office or the hotels where one is staying. The tour is conducted by a guide, and one must adhere to the allocated route in the park for own safety.

A Trip to Bandhavgarh National Park, M.P., Bharat

The **Bandhavgarh National Park** is set amongst the **Vindhya Hills** and the Shadol district, **Madhya Pradesh**. The park derives its name from the most prominent hill fort of the area, which is (mythologically) said to have been given by Lord Rama to his brother Laxman to keep a watch on Lanka. (*Lanka = the island fortress capital of the legendary* ***asura*** *king* ***Ravana*** *in the Ramayana and Mahabharata epics. The Lanka fortress was on a plateau between three peaks, the* ***Trikuta*** *Mountains.*) However, etymologically, the word 'Bandhavgarh' means Bandhav = Brother, Garh = Fort, the fort made for brother Laxman.

This park has an immense **biodiversity**. It has a large breeding population of leopards and various species of deer. It was declared a national park in 1968, covering an area of 437 sq. km. Later, it was declared the **Bandhavgarh Tiger Reserve in 1993**. Presently, it covers an area of 694 sq. km.
November to April is the best time to visit this place and enjoy the wildlife. The nearest airport to the place is **Jabalpur**. The closest town and railway head is Umaria (30 km). Various accommodations are available, including Govt, guest houses, and private hotels. Maruti Gypsies are used to go around the park. One can book these in advance from the Project Tiger Office or the hotel where one is staying.

(45) **You recently visited a Children's Park**, a favorite place for most children in your city. **Write a description of the park** in 100-150 words.

One Day in A Children's Park of Our Locality

'Children's Park' is where all children love to go. We hardly see a child who doesn't love to go to a park. The main attractions of the children's park are the playthings, different rides, boating, and other things. The park in our city is not large, but not so small. The entire park is divided into four areas for different playthings; in the first type, we see rides, sliding, swings, see-saw, and jumping-in ***balloons*** for little children. Type two includes where a boy or a girl can play games like badminton, volleyball, etc. Type three is the part with a swimming pool, where boys and girls between 8 and 18 can learn to swim with the trainers. And lastly, the ***toy train,*** which is almost for all, for children and their parents to go around the park. Apart from all these, there are green areas in the park's center for old parents to play with their kids or grandchildren. Besides, many flower plants, trees, and nurseries are for sale. The staff nursed the plants and trees well, and the park is filled with blooming flowers in all seasons. A flower show is also exhibited in the park in the winter.

(46) **Write an essay on**

My Home City

Balurghat is a small town in West Bengal, India, which I consider my hometown. I grew up there with my parents and have many fond memories. The town is situated on the banks of the Atreyee River and is surrounded by lush greenery, paddy fields, and various water bodies. It is well-connected to other major cities in the state through National Highway 512 and a nearby railway station.

Historically, Balurghat played a significant role in the 'August Movement' in 1942 and the 'Tebhaga Movement' in 1946, pivotal in India's fight for independence from British rule. Despite its historical importance, the city has not seen as much development as others in the region, possibly due to its proximity to the Bangladesh border.

Despite its relatively small size, Balurghat offers various amenities for its residents, including a museum, parks, a super specialty hospital, government offices, a district court, educational institutions, a university, a police station, a railway station, hotels, restaurants, and places of worship for people of different faiths. The city also hosts various religious and cultural festivals from October to November.

Balurghat is known for its clean and peaceful environment, free from pollution, and surrounded by natural beauty. The residents take pride in their simple and peaceful way of life.

(47) **Write an essay on**

My School where I do Read

The school is the temple of learning, where we acquire knowledge on various subjects and engage in different extracurricular activities that help prepare us for our professional careers and social lives. Saidpur B.M.A. High School was established in 1956 on land donated by Baharuddin Mondal, a prominent local farmer. The school was named after his father, Badaruddin Molla, as 'Saidpur Badar Molla Academy High School.' It boasts a well-educated faculty, a large playground, a library, and a cultural committee that organizes various cultural and social events.

The school is tranquil, surrounded by green paddy fields and a large pond to the east, shaded by a large banyan tree. The air is pure and refreshing throughout the year, with comfortable temperatures. We cherish our school not only for its location but also for the dedicated faculty members. We always strive to keep our school campus and classrooms clean, especially before the daily prayer. Mr. Kamal Kr. Our English teacher, Basak, deserves credit for inspiring us to maintain cleanliness and good health.
We have a strong affection for our school, and our teachers effectively and creatively guide us.

(48) **Write an essay on**

Taj Mahal

The Taj Mahal is the love symbol of the great Mughal emperor of Agra. It was built using white marble and over a thousand pearls and stones, giving it an attractive and fantastic look that shines in the moonlight. Rabindranath Tagore called it *"A Dream in Marble."* It is an absolute heaven on earth and is mentioned as a UNESCO World Heritage Site. It was built by the great Mughal emperor Shah Jahan in memory of his

dead wife, Mumtaz Mahal. It is considered that he had loved her so much and became so sad after her death. He started living without food and water. He decided to keep all her memories in front of his eyes and began to build the immortal Taj Mahal in front of the Agra Fort, which now brings millions of visitors worldwide every year.
The Taj Mahal took many years to complete after its construction began. This historical monument symbolizes Shah Jahan's love for his wife, Mumtaz Mahal. The Taj Mahal's surrounding environment is natural and attractive. It is located on the bank of the Yamuna River in Agra, UP. The Taj Mahal was built using royal designs based on the ideas of many artists, architects, etc. Many decorative grasses and trees enhance the beauty and fragrance of the environment.
There are also some charming water fountains in the middle of the cemented footpath in front of the Taj Mahal building. These lovely water fountains make the entry to the grand mausoleum. The Taj Mahal is one of the best and most beautiful tourist destinations in Bharat. Its great artistic charm attracts millions of visitors from around the world annually. It is the most fascinating monument of Bharat and has been chosen as the world's seventh wonder.

6. ESSAYS on EVENT & SITUATION (Descriptive Writing)

Any description of an event should include factual details. While writing about an event, the following points should be kept in mind.

- As the event is described after completion, one must *use past tense*.
- *All the event facts must be included* while writing the description.
- It is always *better not to include personal opinions or comments* while describing an event. (***better to be*** **'Descriptive Writing'**)

Organizing a Robot-Making Competition

(49) You recently participated in a 'Robot Making' event organized at your school. Read the following points and describe the event in an essay.

(Participants from as many as 30 schools in the city—robots made by each team—presented their different functions—were awarded the best prize.)

At our school, we recently participated in a thrilling Robot-Making Competition that brought together 30 schools from across the city. Being a member of the Robotics Club, I had the honor of representing my school alongside my classmate Nil in this exciting event.
Upon arrival, each group of students was provided with a unique set of tools and components to construct their robot. It was fascinating to see how each group's robot differed due to the distinct materials they received. With only two hours on the clock, we busily set to work, assembling our robot, which we envisioned to be able to play music and carry out essential household tasks like making beds and washing dishes. The atmosphere was buzzing with energy and creativity as each group worked to bring their robots to life. One group nearby focused on constructing a running robot capable of participating in races, adding to the excitement in the air.

In the end, the first prize award went to the impressive running robot created by the neighboring group. Their efficiency in assembling the robot and outstanding performance made them the well-deserved winners. However, as all the robots were completed, the auditorium was a spectacle to behold, filled with a diverse array of robots showcasing their unique abilities. Our robot secured the second prize, and all participants received individual certificates to commemorate their hard work and dedication.

The event was graced by a distinguished Chief Guest, a Professor of Robotics from the renowned University of Technology at Kharagpur IIT. His inspiring speech left us feeling motivated and encouraged to pursue robotics in the future, marking the perfect conclusion to a memorable and inspiring competition.

Write a short paragraph on the 'Robot-Making Competition':
We recently participated in a Robot-Making Competition with 30 schools. The competition was held at our school campus. Each group received a set of tools to construct their robot. Our robot, designed to play music and handle household tasks, earned us a second prize. The winning robot was a running robot, which impressed everyone. The event featured a distinguished Chief Guest, a Professor of Robotics, whose inspiring speech motivated us to pursue robotics further in the future.

Watching a Cricket Tournament

(50) **You recently witnessed the World Cup Bharat-South Africa Cricket match in Nagpur**. From beginning to end, it was a nail-biting match. Describe the event in 150 words.

I vividly remember the electrifying atmosphere at World Cup matches, especially with the passionate Bharatiya crowd. The excitement of watching the game was only part of the experience; the passionate enthusiasm of the crowd added another layer of thrill. I had the incredible opportunity to attend the last Bharat-South Africa match in Nagpur, Bharat. I made a memorable trip from Kolkata to catch the match, and the stadium was packed. Every delivery from the Bharatiya bowlers and every run scored by the Bharatiyas elicited thunderous cheers, enthusiastic shouts, relentless applause, and a sea of flags waving throughout the match—a truly unforgettable sight.

Rohit Sharma's phenomenal 111-run performance captivated the crowd during the match, but the atmosphere shifted when Kohli was bowled just after reaching his half-century. The energy was palpable, and witnessing it all was an absolute delight. Additionally, Umran Malik's outstanding three-wicket haul added to the excitement. Despite the valiant efforts, South Africa emerged victorious, and Bharat secured the third position in the last World Cup.

A Dance Performance I Saw

(51) **Write a few sentences about a dance performance that you have seen recently.**

I witnessed a mesmerizing dance performance at Balurghat Maidan last week. It was a captivating Chhau dance presented by a group of artists from Purulia. They all donned masks, swayed to the rhythm, brandished weapons, and leaped in unison with the music, all without uttering a single word. I particularly liked the diverse drumbeats (such as Dhol, Dhamsa, and Dhak) and the soul-stirring flute melodies accompanying the dance's rhythm. The performance depicted gripping battle scenes between gods and demons, culminating in the triumph of the Goddess over the Demon (symbolizing the victory of good over evil).

'How to Achieve Success'

(52) You recently attended a seminar on '**How to Achieve Success**'. Using the clues below, describe the event in 100-150 words.

Tips for Success:

- Do not be fixated with results; enjoy the journey that leads you to them.
- Always measure your improvements and work to better yourself in all spheres.
- Do not wait for the opportunity to knock on the door. However, if it does, make the most of it.
- Fame and money flow in with passion and perseverance.
- Measure your decisions and build a strong determination.

On Monday, our school hosted a seminar titled "How to Achieve Success," which drew 600 people from diverse backgrounds. Five distinguished speakers delivered speeches and shared valuable insights. They emphasized that success should be viewed as a personal journey of continuous improvement rather than a comparison. They stressed the need to create opportunities rather than waiting for them to appear and highlighted the importance of perseverance. The speakers also emphasized the significance of teamwork, asserting that individual success is intertwined with the success of the team and the organization. Attending the seminar has made me feel better equipped to handle everyday challenges, marking the first tangible benefit I've gained from the event.

'Career Fair'

(53) Your school organized a 'Career Fair' this year. As many as 30 Institutes put up their stalls. Some participants included NIFT, NID, IIPM, Computer Academy, etc. The school also invited career counselors. Write a descriptive writing of the event.

The Career Fair is an annual event at our school that provides a platform for students from classes 9 to 12 to meet with experts from various fields and learn about their career options after completing the 10th grade, 12th grade, and graduation. The fair featured experts from fields such as medicine, engineering, fashion, design, architecture, and film and representatives from institutions like NIFT, NID, IIPM, and Computer Academy. Notable participants included Mr. Jagmohan Chawla, a Consultant Ophthalmologist, and Ms. Prema, a Pacific Beach Elementary School teacher. The event also included books and food stalls. Parents were welcome to attend and had the opportunity to interact with the experts and gather information about the different career options available. The fair was open to students in grades 9 to 12 and their parents.

Flood Relief Camp

(54) Read the clues or pointers given below, and write down a paragraph (descriptive) on the following topic:

[*Floods in UP: heavy rain, a breach in the dam, large tracts inundated, standing crops devastated, relief operations, army, NGOs, camp for flood victims.*]

During my visit to the camps run by local NGOs, I was deeply moved by the plight of the people affected by the devastating floods in our region. The local NGOs had already provided help and relief to the flood victims. I visited the camp with the NSS team from our college.

Heavy rains caused a breach in an eastern UP dam on the Gandak River, resulting in the inundation of many villages. Villagers lost their homes, cattle, and standing crops. Consequently, they became homeless and helpless. Many individuals are reported to be missing. Those who survived were in a miserable state. As soon as the weather permitted, the army brought the survivors to these relief camps. Our main task was to assist the army in bringing the survivors to the relief camps and to do our best to save their lives and cattle from the flooded areas. With the government's help, the NGOs provided the victims with food, medicines, and clothes.

I witnessed the misery and hopelessness in the eyes of the flood victims. Farmers and laborers who once led dignified lives were now reduced to near beggars. Poverty was etched on their faces, and diseases were ready to pounce on the unfortunate. The plight of the children was the most tragic of all. They were confused and frightened, having lost the battle of life before it even began.

Benefits of Early Morning Exercise

(55) **Write a paragraph (in about 100-150 words) on the benefits of early morning exercise using the following points:**

[good for health—early morning sky—fresh air—keeps us fit and healthy—one hour's exercise—keeps one active throughout the day— conclusion.]

Remember that daily exercise in the early morning is essential for staying healthy and fit. Doing so for an hour or even half an hour can set you up for a full, active day. The morning air is fresh and pollution-free, making it the perfect time for exercises such as morning walks, running two kilometers, free-hand exercises, or jogging. Doctors even recommend morning exercise for their patients due to its health benefits. In addition to the physical advantages, morning exercise sets a positive tone for the entire day, helping us to stay active and energetic in our daily activities. Regardless of age, everyone should prioritize waking up early for exercise suitable for their age. The saying "Early to bed, early to rise makes a man healthy, wealthy, and wise" emphasizes the importance of sleeping, waking up early, and engaging in daily exercise to maintain a healthy body and mind. A healthy mind supports proper thinking and promotes wisdom.

Pay Attention to Street Dogs

(56) Write a paragraph within 150 words on how you plan to take care of **street dogs.** Use the following hints:

[Indifference towards street dogs—cruel actions by some—necessity of looking after them—ways of taking care of the dogs—conclusion.]

The first animal to become our pet and friend was a dog. Today, however, street dogs are often neglected and mistreated. Some people even go so far as to throw stones at them or beat them whenever they can. Due to a lack of food, shelter, care, and security, these animals suffer significantly from birth to death. However, they only require a little attention from us. We can make a huge difference by providing them with food daily and shelter in an unused corner or shade of our house. Street dogs are naturally gentle and loyal and only bite if provoked or made to feel insecure. They also bark to alert us of strangers, helping to keep our neighborhoods safe. These animals can be our true friends for life with a little care, sympathy, and food.

7. ESSAYS on EXPERIENCE & IDEAS (Narrative Writing)

The Game I Like Most

(57) **Sample 2: Write a short paragraph on 'The Game I like most. Here, it is on 'Cricket'.**

Step 1: Give a Title → The Game I Like Most- Cricket

Step 2: Make an Outline → Cricket is a historic Game. It is Popular in Bharat. I play it with my friends on Sundays. I also watch cricket on TV.

Step 3: Expanding the outlines or points into more Sentences to make a paragraph: →

Cricket, The Game I Like Most

Cricket is a historic game. It has been played for over a hundred years. It began in England, and the British brought it to Bharat. It is now the most popular game in Bharat.

I play it with my friends in a local playground in the afternoon. I enjoy the game very much. I also enjoy watching cricket games, national and international, on Television with my elders. These days, one-day Internationals and Twenty-Twenty matches are popular. They are thrilling. I watch them, especially on TV. We feel proud whenever Bharat wins a game.

My Favorite Fruit

(58) Write a descriptive writing about your favorite fruit. Suppose an orange is your favorite fruit, among others,

Step 1: Give a Title to your paragraph - My Favorite Fruit
Step 2: Describe the fruit with describing words: write the name of the fruit you like most, its size, color, type, and use; add as many points as necessary, or you want to describe your favorite fruit, like, My favorite fruit is orange. It is orange in color. It looks like a circle. It has a peel. It is a juicy fruit for making juices, jams, and sweets.
Step 3: Mention the reason, 'Why do you like it?' For example, I like this fruit because it is rich in Vitamin C.
Step 4: Write a Concluding line: It is a seasonal fruit. It is suitable for health. Thus, the complete paragraph would be like,

My Favorite Fruit

My absolute favorite fruit is the orange. This vibrant fruit boasts a brilliant orange hue and a circular shape, with a rigid yet yielding peel that encases its juicy, succulent flesh. Oranges are extensively used to create refreshing juices, flavorful jams, and delectable sweets. Not only do I adore the citrusy taste, but I also appreciate the high Vitamin C content and the health benefits it offers. Furthermore, its availability is tied to certain seasons, making each experience of enjoying an orange all the more special. (86 words)

My Favorite Story Book

(59) Write a short paragraph on 'Your Favorite Story Book'.

Title: '**My Favorite Story Book'**

For the rest, you may follow the guide in the form of questions:

a) Which story do you like?
b) Who has written it?
c) What's about the story?
d) What is the story?
e) How do you feel?
f) Why do you like it very much?
g) Any message for others?

Now, if we arrange the answers to the above questions:

a) The Ugly Duckling
b) Written by Hans Christian Anderson
c) Hans Christian Anderson wrote beautiful fairy tales.
d) The story is about a little ugly duckling who was ignored by everyone earlier, but with time, the ugly duckling grew into a beautiful swan. Everyone began to admire him.
e) Felt happy and excited!
f) Has a happy ending.
g) Everything will turn out right if you believe in yourself.

Now, read the complete paragraph.

My Favorite Story Book

My favorite storybook is 'The Ugly Duckling.' It was written by the famous writer Hans Christian Anderson. He wrote beautiful fairy tales for children. The story is about a little duckling. Everyone thought he was ugly. His parents, brothers, and sisters ignored him because he was different. He did not look like them, and he did not sound like them. Everyone made fun of him. He was lonely and sad. Time passed, and soon, the ugly duckling grew into a beautiful swan. He was not an ugly duckling anymore. Everyone began to admire his beauty, and he was no longer ignored by anyone. This is my favorite storybook because it has a happy ending. I like happy endings, where everything should turn out right at the end.

Now, study an example of essay writing. Note carefully how it is different from a paragraph:

A Visit to the Zoo

(60) **Write a narrative essay on 'A Visit to the Zoo'.**

Now, when we write about 'visiting a zoo,' it will include our own experience so that the writing will be narrative. But we may also describe an animal in the zoo with words so that it would be descriptive, too. So, narrative writing does not mean there are no describing words in it, but it adds the author's opinion and more paragraphs than one. A piece of writing may be at a time both descriptive and narrative. The terms are only to understand how your writing is, not more than that it has any goal.

Step 1: Write a Title: **A Visit to the Zoo**

Step 2: Question Words:

- → When do you visit a zoo?
- → Where do you visit a zoo?
- → With whom do you visit?
- → What preparation did you make before visiting the zoo?

Step 3: Brainstorming technique:

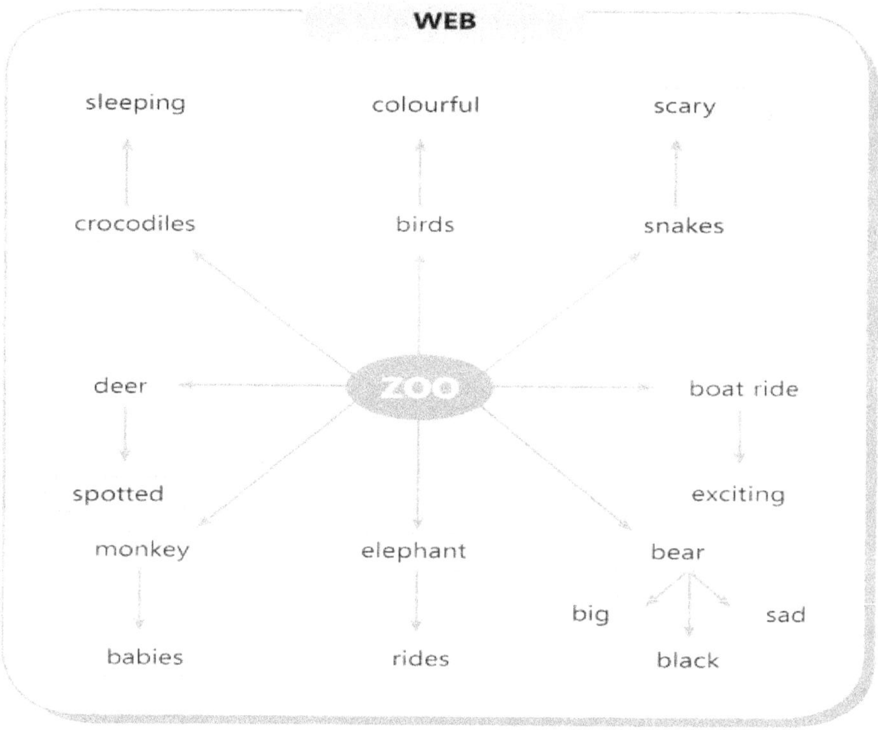

The brainstorming technique helps to get answers to the following questions:

→ What have you seen there?
→ Describe each, like their color, size, specialty, if any
→ What are they doing? What are your interactions, your experiences?
→ When did you leave the zoo?
→ Your overall feeling or your experience in the concluding line.

Step 4: We may form an Outline too before writing the paragraph:

I visited last Saturday – with my parents – watched crocodiles, monkeys, and bears – took refreshments – watched elephants, birds, and snakes – took a boat ride – left the zoo in time–and enjoyed it a lot.

Step 5: Now develop the narrative essay on 'A Visit to Zoo.'

Title → **'A Visit to Zoo'**

→ *Answering the question words.*

I visited the zoo last Saturday with my parents and younger sister. The zoo is located in Alipore, Kolkata. My mother packed some sandwiches and fruits in a picnic basket. We left the lodge at 8:30 a.m. to reach the zoo before it opened at 10:30, but we reached it by 9:15 a.m. We bought tickets and entered the zoo.

→ With the help of brainstorming techniques, we may form an outline as well as develop our experiences into independent sentences to form paragraphs, as,

We went to see the crocodiles first. They were sleeping in the sun. Then we visited the deer - some were big, some were small, and there were spotted deer. After that, I ran off with my sister to see the monkeys. Many baby monkeys were playing with each other, which made us laugh. We spent some time watching them and even fed them bananas. Next, we went to see the bear. There was only one bear in the zoo when I visited. It was big and black, and it looked pretty lonely. Then we found a nice place to sit because my sister was hungry. My mother took out the sandwiches, and they were delicious. After eating, I saw the birds while my mother stayed behind. I saw different kinds of birds, some beautiful in color. While watching the birds, an elephant came along with people sitting on its back. I felt sorry for it because so many people took rides on it.
My father wanted to see the snakes next, but I don't like snakes, so I stayed far from the glass jars with my mom. Before leaving the zoo, we rode a boat and saw different-colored fish swimming. I almost fell into the water while looking over the side, and my sister couldn't stop laughing at me. We left the zoo at 4:30 p.m.

→ Give a Concluding statement, like the following:

We enjoyed our visit to the zoo and hope to come again soon. I also hope the people in charge can get more animals and birds before my next visit.

(61) **Write a paragraph in 150 words using the given hints. Give a title to the paragraph:**
[**Hints:** returning from the educational excursion by bus—night journey—sudden breakdown—tire punctured—had to wait for two hours—at a lonely place—tire fixed—back home.]

An Unforgettable Night

Last summer, we returned from an educational trip by bus from Hazarduari to Balurghat. It was an exciting and educational tour, and we were all reflecting on our experiences in silence when suddenly, we heard a loud noise, felt a jolt, and the bus stopped. It was midnight, and we were informed that the bus had a puncture and there was no nearby garage for repairs. Many of us got off the bus into the lonely, moonlit night. The summer breeze felt pleasant under the starry sky. However, some of my classmates panicked, thinking it might be a bus robbery, which caused some commotion among the passengers. After about two hours of excitement, the driver and his assistant fixed the tire. We finally resumed our journey almost at dawn. It was a memorable experience to spend a night under the starry sky, and it will always stay with me.

(62) **Write a few sentences about your journey from your home to school. You can use the following hints:**
*(**hints:** distance between home and school—modes of traveling—important landmarks—things can be seen in the course of the journey—the most exciting part of the journey.)*

Route Map to My School

The distance from my home to school is .... k.m./meters. Generally, I travel to my school by/on .... (***bus/cycle/walk***). There is a .... (***temple/***

mosque/ large banyan tree) beside my school. When I go to my school, I see .... (***endless green field/many shops and buildings /office houses and vehicles***) in the course of my journey every day. The most exciting part of my journey is the .... (***long straight road /curved path/stony pathway***) that seems most exciting to .... (look fixedly/drive fast /walk challenging) to reach my school in time.

To be noted: *Complete the paragraph choosing the correct options or make another.*

(63) **Write a paragraph in 100 words to describe yourself using the following hints: (Hints:** *name and age, place of life, name of school reading, hobby, likes and dislikes, and what you want to be when you grow up.)*

Describing Myself

My name is Pritam, and I am an eleven-year-old boy. I live in Saidpur village in the district of Dakshin Dinajpur, which is also my home district. I study at Saidpur B.M.A. High School. Drawing is my favorite hobby, and I also enjoy reading story books, particularly science fiction. I do not like watching television or playing games on my mobile. However, I love playing football with my friends in the village playground. My idols are Kalpana Chawla and A.P.J. Abdul Kalam. As I grow up, I dream of becoming an astronaut and being the first person to land on Mars.

My Dream / The Goal of Life

(64) Write an essay on 'your dream'. Of course, it is not an event but a situation you are thinking of in your future, how it would be, etc.

Dreams are a vision of the future. Everyone has dreams and pursues them with sincerity and perseverance. A.P.J. Abdul Kalam said, "Dreams are not what you see in sleep. They are the things that don't let you sleep." This quote highlights the idea of pursuing our goals.

Everyone should have a dream in life, a vision that they must follow with utmost effort. Like others, I also have a dream. I have nurtured it since college. I aspire to write and publish my own books.

To achieve this, I am working hard, reading top writers' stories, novels, and books to understand how they express their views and thoughts. It has become clear that writing a book requires personal experience, knowledge, and the skill of using imagination. First-hand experience makes the task easier, but knowing how to express it is even more important. It requires extensive knowledge, a super imaginative power, and the skill of presenting thoughts or ideas in words. I am not sure if I possess these qualities, but I am determined to pursue my dream with sincerity and perseverance until it comes true one day.

I often recall Kazi Nazrul Islam's line, "We shall overcome, we shall overcome someday," when standing on the beach and looking at the distant sea. I cherish and strive to live by the sayings—' Where there is a will, there's a way' and 'God helps those who help themselves.' I believe that with determination, I will fulfill my dream one day.

What I want to be /The Goal of Life

(65) What do you want to be? Give reasons for your choice. Write a few sentences. Begin like this:

(hints: I want to be a....)

I want to be an aerospace engineer like Sunita Williams. I want to fly like them once when I grow up. The infinite sky, the stars, and the planets often welcome me madly, particularly at night when I look at them. If I can be an aerospace engineer, I must apply to include my name for such an adventure to the higher authority. I am eagerly waiting for a rocket launch and waiting for my turn one day. How would it be if I were the first man on Mars or somewhere where still no man lands? Sunita Williams and Kalpana Chawla are my ideals, and I have studied them extensively.

How Looks My Locality at Dawn

(66) **Using the following points given, write a paragraph in 100-150 words on how your locality looks like at dawn:**

[Your place of stay—early morning sky—description of the nature around—sounds heard—reasons for enjoyment—conclusion.]

Like millions of other children in Bharat, I am a village boy. My village is located in the center of West Bengal, about 50 km from the capital city of Balurghat. It is a calm and pleasant place, with beautiful views of nature, clear skies, and pure air. The village is near the bank of a small river called Tangan, where I used to swim and dive to find pearls in my boyhood days.

Every day, I wake up with my father at dawn, and we walk along the village's wet, muddy paths. We are greeted by a gentle and mild breeze, and we can hear the cries of animals and the songs of birds. I love watching the sunrise almost every day as it emerges from the horizon at the end of our village. I enjoy the sight and sounds of birds chirping, goats bleating, and cows mooing. I am proud to be a village boy, like millions of others in my motherland.

(67) Write six connected sentences about your experience of seeing the night sky. You may use the following points:

(hints: time of see—place from where you see—how the sky looks—other things that you see—sounds of the night—your feelings.)

Experience of Seeing Night Sky

I often go to the roof of our house in the evening. I see the sky full of stars; some shine brighter than others, while some twinkle feebly. I love the natural lighting of the night sky. I also see some birds, like owls and bats. Are there any others? Some crickets chirp, and an owl hoots, making everything more mysterious, and they transport me from my world. Soon, I find myself flying with them. I fly over the horizon, over the hills and trees, and this goes on until my mother comes to wake me from my trance.

My first ever Sea Voyage on a Small Boat

(68) Imagine you are on an open sea in a boat with waves rising all around you. Would you feel scared or excited? Write a paragraph in about 100 words describing your experience of the sea voyage:

The Thrills at Sea

I remember the moment vividly. I had always longed for a sea voyage since watching a movie about it on TV. One day, I found myself in the middle of an open sea on a small boat, with waves rising and crashing all around me. How did I get here? I felt a mix of intimidation and excitement. A long-cherished wish was finally coming true. The immense power of the waves reminded me of the unstoppable forces of nature and the sea. The boat rose and fell with the waves, sending a rush of adrenaline through me. The salty air filled my lungs, and the wind whipped through my hair. It was a thrilling and daring adventure to be out there. Despite the fear, there was an undeniable thrill in embarking on this little boat, an adventure that would leave a lasting mark on my soul. But suddenly, a large wave hit the boat, and I woke up.

Waiting for a Good News to Come

(69) ***Suppose you have been waiting for good news. Write a paragraph in about 100 words on your experience of waiting.*** Keep in mind the following points to follow up in the section:
(the news you are waiting for, what you did while waiting, whether the news came, and your feelings.)

Waiting for a Good News to Come

I eagerly awaited the news that I would soon have my younger brother or sister. The anticipation filled me with both excitement and impatience. While waiting, I had been occupied with thoughts of what it would be like to have a sibling. I imagined the fun we would have, the adventures we would share, and the bond we would develop. Each passing day felt like a step closer to the arrival of our new family member. When the news finally came that it was a baby boy, my heart burst with joy and excitement. I could not wait any longer to meet my little sibling, so I went to the nursing home to say 'hello' to my younger brother. A new chapter of our lives began after that.

When I was a tea-bearer

(70) Suppose you had to obey someone's orders from morning to night. You were not allowed to act according to your own will. Write a paragraph of about 100 words describing your feelings in this situation.

The Bondage Part of My Life

I am from a poor family. Feeding five adults and three kids, including a sick grandparent, was not easy for my parents. My father was an auto rickshaw driver, and my mother worked as a cook in local households. For some time, I worked in a tea shop near the village. The work was not very difficult, but there was little freedom for the children living there. I felt that being poor was a curse. As a tea shop worker, I had to follow the shop owner's orders from morning to night. I had no freedom to play, go to school, study, or even watch television on holidays. It was a dark time in my life that I spent a whole year. Although that time has passed, it still haunts me during lonely hours. It was a life of curse! I hope that no other child has to go through such an experience.

If I were a Merlin, the Wise Counselor to King Arthur

(71) Imagine you are Merlin, King Arthur's wise counselor. Write a paragraph of about 100 words on the advice you would give the king in his times of trouble.

What I would suggest to King Arthur

To the noble King Arthur,

As a loyal servant of the kingdom, I humbly present some suggestions for your consideration. The people of the kingdom are eagerly awaiting the restoration of the prosperous days of your late father. Therefore, I urge you to prioritize establishing law and order in the country. It is also essential to immediately appoint a network of loyal spies throughout the realm to gather crucial information and provide timely warnings about any potential conspiracies or threats from the barons, nobles, or enemies.

Furthermore, ensuring peace and prosperity among our people and protecting them from oppressive barons is imperative. To achieve this, a group of honest, fearless, and loyal knights and a formidable army will be indispensable. Your selection of knights should be based on their ability to help the vulnerable and bring justice to the kingdom, ultimately fostering happiness and prosperity.

I hope these suggestions are of value as you lead the kingdom toward a brighter future.

Sincerely,

[Your Name].

A Day with My Talking Bird

(72) **Suppose you have a bird that talks and plays with you.** Write a paragraph in about 100 words on how you spent a day with the bird during the last summer vacation:

A Day with My Talking Bird

I have a pigeon that can talk like a parrot and play with me, which is quite surprising. I rescued the bird when it was just a baby, saving it from its kind who wanted to kill it to take over its nest in our White Home. It has grown quite a bit, and one day, it started talking like a parrot. Now we are great friends. Last summer, I spent an entire day with my bird. It chirps, talks, and mimics my words, and we have playful conversations. We play hide-and-seek and chase each other. It takes long flights over trees and shares with me what it sees. It perches on my shoulder, and we share fruits and drinks from different pots as we walk in nature. We had a fantastic day of fun together in the nearby forest.

An Autobiography of a Broken Cycle

(73) An author's personal account (description) is called an autobiography. Here, write an autobiographical paragraph about a broken bicycle:

An Autobiography of a Broken Bicycle

I am a broken bicycle. I can recall my earlier days when I was young and new to my owner, a young boy. He would ride on me and go to his school every day. Riding on me, he often visited his friends in nearby villages. I was then his favorite. The young boy is now a grown-up man, and my place is in the corner of a storeroom in the house, along with other waste materials. Now, he or his father, who bought me, hardly remembers. My place for their riding has now been replaced with a broom. Silently, I count my last days in the shade.

Alone in a Railway Station

(74) Suppose you find yourself alone in a railway station at night. Write a paragraph in about 100 words describing your experience.

Alone in a Railway Station

I am Peter. I was returning alone from my maternal uncle's house in Siliguri once. It was only half past eight when I reached Siliguri station, but due to heavy rain and cloudy skies, it felt like midnight. No other passengers were around, just benches, chairs, and a few dim lights. Memories of the events from 'Midnight's Express,' which I read in class VIII, came to my mind, and I began to shiver in fear. I remembered my uncle's warning, as he had advised me not to travel that night. I regretted not listening to him. Suddenly, a voice startled me. I turned around to see a man in a black coat asking, "Where are you headed?" I replied, "Balurghat." He checked his watch and said, "Only half an hour more." Thankfully, the train arrived on time. I quickly boarded and felt relieved when I saw many other passengers in the compartment.

A Moonlit Night in a Forest Guest House

(75) Suppose you spent a moonlit night in a forest guest house. Write a paragraph of about 100 words on your experience. Mention the sounds that you heard and sights you observed there.

A Moonlit Night in a Forest Guest House

I spent a night in a forest guest house I had longed to visit. It was thrilling and peaceful, just like my last summer vacation.

I convinced my parents to let me stay alone while they stayed in another room. The night was quiet, and the interplay of light and shadow made everything more mysterious. Suddenly, I heard knocking on the door. I was afraid it might be a ghost. I cried out, "Who's there?" but received no reply. I thought it might be a wild animal. The knocking happened again, and I mustered my courage to open the door slowly. No one was there to greet me or check if everything was okay. I felt less scared and sat in a wooden rocking chair, listening to crickets chirping, owls hooting, and more. I closed my eyes and soon fell into sound sleep. It was the first time I spent a whole night alone in the lap of nature, feeling blessed and at peace.

An Autobiography of an Owl

(76) Write an autobiography of an owl and how it enjoys the night in about 100 words:

An Autobiography of an Owl

I am an owl, slightly big and gray in color. People call me a screeching owl, although I do not constantly screech. I live in a dark forest, in a hole in a tree or between branches where light hardly disturbs my sleep during the day. On the moonlit night, one may find me sitting on a branch of a large tree. I am lucky to be a nocturnal bird. The forest looks beautiful at night, and I enjoy the play of light and shadow in the moonlight. I often wonder how people and other animals bear the sun's shining, bright, and burning light during the daytime. When I see a mouse scampering about, I feel very happy at the sight of my food. The clear sky, the moon, the fragrance of night flowers, the silent forest, and my pleasure make me hoot.

A Song I Like Most

(77) Write a paragraph of about 100 words about a song you like very much. Mention the reasons you like the song.

My Favorite Song

One of my favorite songs is "The Nights" by Avicii. The uplifting and inspirational track never fails to ignite a sense of adventure within me. From the energetic beats to the catchy melodies and heart-touching lyrics, every element of the song emits a sense of positivity and optimism. Its lyrics tell a story of chasing dreams, taking risks, and creating everlasting memories. "The Nights" encourages me to live a life to the fullest and make the most of our experiences. Every time I listen to this song, it fills me with joy and the desire to live my life to the fullest. The empowering and uplifting soundtrack of "The Nights" solidifies its place as one of my all-time favorites.

8. ESSAYS on PROVERBS, SLOGANS

(78) **Write an essay on**

A Friend in Need is a Friend Indeed

Student life is precious, and it is a time to have lots of fun and make good friends. Good friends may come into one's life at any phase, depending on one's nature, qualities such as trustworthiness and honesty, and where two people's attitudes meet.

Everyone needs good friends. A good friend is not just someone to play or act with, but much more. A good friend can help and guide you in need. This relationship should be mutual, just like friendship. If you expect help from your friends, be trustworthy to them as well. Learn to give - your love, hard work, and devotion - and expect nothing in return. Enjoy the journey, and the experience will be wonderful.

Life has its ups and downs, joys and sorrows. When we enjoy the good times, we must be prepared for the bad ones. In difficult times, good friends are invaluable. We need good friends to help us through the tough times. "A Friend in Need is a Friend Indeed" holds during difficult phases of life. Fake friends fade away, while true friends light up our path. With good friends, we can pass through sad times happily.

True friends are of great importance in one's life. Humans are social beings and cannot thrive alone. This is why we have various relationships - with parents, spouses, children, relatives, and friends. Each relationship is unique and holds a different significance. Friends are essential for sharing everything, especially things young adults may not share with their parents. Good friends give us good memories, so we should cherish them forever.

(79) **Write an essay on**

Beti Bachao Beti Padhao

Prime Minister Narendra Modi of Bharat introduced the 'Beti Bachao Beti Padhao' scheme to address the pressing issues related to the welfare of girl children. The initiative, which translates to 'Save Girls, and Give Them Education', aims to bolster the number of girl children, curb female feticide, and provide them with essential security and education across the nation. It was launched on 22nd January 2015 in Panipat, Haryana. The scheme was implemented in response to the alarming decline in the ratio of girls to male children (0 to 6 years) from 945/1000 in 1991 to 918/1000 in 2011.

The scheme endeavors to combat female feticide and ensure girls' overall well-being in Bharat. It seeks to empower girls by granting them social and financial independence while striving to mitigate gender discrimination nationwide.

The ultimate goal of the 'Beti Bachao Beti Padhao scheme is to create a society where no girl child faces the threats of violence, educational deprivation, or insecurity due to socio-economic factors. This comprehensive initiative aspires to bring about positive, lasting changes in the lives of girl children throughout Bharat.

(80) **Write an essay on**

Cleanliness is next to Godliness

The well-known adage "Cleanliness is next to Godliness" is a profound saying initially attributed to English cleric John Wesley in 1778. This proverb underscores the significance of cleanliness in a person's life. It suggests that just as individuals diligently pursue religious devotion, they should prioritize body, mind, and soul cleanliness. Essentially, it conveys the idea that pure and wholesome people are close to God.

The proverb effectively equates cleanliness with godliness. Cleanliness refers to being physically tidy and maintaining clean surroundings, while godliness denotes devout religiousness.

In this context, Godliness implies spiritual purity achieved through maintaining personal and environmental cleanliness. When we uphold cleanliness, we rid our bodies and minds of malevolent thoughts and negativity, drawing closer to divinity.

This adage advocates for individuals to uphold personal and environmental cleanliness to nurture a healthy lifestyle. It also proposes that the path to godliness is intertwined with mind, soul, and body balance. By adopting clean habits and maintaining hygiene, one can inch closer to spiritual purity and closeness to God. Furthermore, the saying resonates with the popular notion that "Purity is the way to God," emphasizing the value of cleanliness and instilling a sense of devotion toward maintaining personal and environmental hygiene. A clean mind and body are not only desirable to God but are also revered by society.

(81) **Write an essay on**

Digital Bharat

In today's fast-paced world, keeping up with technological advances is essential. The "Digital Bharat" initiative, launched by the government of Bharat on July 1, 2015, aims to transform the country into a digitally empowered nation. The initiative, observed during the first week of July as "Digital Week," encompasses various governmental departments like IT, education, agriculture, and more, all working together to achieve this ambitious objective.

Led and planned by the Ministry of Communications and Information Technology, Bharat, this initiative presents an unprecedented opportunity for Bharat and its organizations to embrace digital transformation nationally. The initial phase includes plans by state governments to provide high-speed internet connections to nearly 250,000 villages and residential areas across the country. The "Bharat Broadband Network Limited (BBNL)" involvement in this project has been essential and commendable.

The digital Bharat initiative promises streamlined processes and increased efficiency by digitizing data across government and public departments. This will ultimately reduce paperwork, save manpower, and accelerate progress. Collaboration between the government and private sectors is crucial to the success of this project. The extensive rollout of high-speed networks to numerous villages is poised to uplift these areas and propel them into digitally equipped regions.

As a result of this initiative, cities, towns, and villages across Bharat will become more technologically advanced. The project is anticipated to be completed by 2019, with significant investments from leading national and international companies. This visionary initiative sets the stage for Bharat to establish itself as a force to be reckoned with in the digital world.

(82) **Write an essay on**

Education is the most potent weapon.

Introduction: Nelson Mandela was right when he stated, "Education is the most potent weapon you can utilize to transform the world." Yes, the solution to any issue lies in education. Education is essential for progress and success in life, society, or nation.
We can use education to increase economic and sociological quality of life. Education is power, no doubt, and can transform our entire lives. It is a gesture where you accept knowledge and then give methodical directions in return, ranging from promoting gender equality to eliminating poverty.

Importance Of Education: You can understand the importance of education by reading the following points I will discuss.

1. Helps Us Become Better Citizens: Despite being the most sophisticated and advanced species on Earth, humans are merely creatures with the capacity for rational thought and behavior. However, a person cannot develop that rationalism within themselves without education. So, education helps us reason, make the right decisions, and become better and more responsible citizens.

2. Enhances The Nation's Progress: Educated people are the foundation of any nation. If you are educated, you can distinguish between right and wrong. You are reasonably knowledgeable about the available resources and the best ways to use them. So, you will work to improve your country and, ultimately, your country.

3. Ensures A Promising Future: Education is the key to leading a contented and prosperous life. It assists us in identifying our hidden abilities and talents, which we can use to advance our careers, find work, and ensure our promising future. So, with education, you can have a successful profession and achieve your professional and personal goals.

How Does Education Influence Society? Learning is a lifelong process that never ends. New ideas arise with learning; before you know it, you question previous concepts and beliefs. Your environment and personality have changed, which makes it easier for you to communicate with one another, and feel free to share your thoughts. So, education aids in shaping one's perspective on life and their ideas reflected in the society where they live.

What Are The Ways Education Bring Change In Society? Let me now tell you how education brings about change in our society.

1. Provides Knowledge: The first thing you receive through education is knowledge of the world around you and the modifications that can be made to improve it.

2. Help To Solve Problems And Over Different Social Evils: Education provides information. Information gives knowledge. Knowledge develops understanding, which helps to solve different problems in society and the world—whether in the economy, society, medicine, or politics.

Education Is The Key To Society's Success: Education is the most potent weapon. One child, one teacher, one book, and one pen have the power to change the world. The only remedy is education. First, put education.

Conclusion: Therefore, after reviewing all of the aforementioned examples of how education can be used as a weapon, we can all conclude that education is a great equalizer that helps raise living standards, benefits communities, and even protects people from abuse and unrealistic expectations. Improving educational access and quality leads to more excellent outcomes at all levels.

(83) **Write an essay on**

Health is Wealth

Certainly! Maintaining good health is integral to living a fulfilling life. It is often regarded as the most precious possession in a person's life. Individuals must adhere to a well-rounded approach to attaining and upholding good health. This involves regular physical exercise, practicing yoga and meditation, consuming a balanced and nutritious diet, nurturing positive thoughts, observing personal hygiene, and ensuring timely health check-ups at least twice a year. Adequate rest and sleep are also indispensable components of sustaining good health.

Good health contributes to overall well-being and minimizes the frequency of medical expenses, as it diminishes the need for regular visits to the doctor. Therefore, adopting a disciplined lifestyle is crucial to avoid the burden of continual healthcare interventions. The adage "Health is Wealth" epitomizes the essence of good health, as it propels a person towards success and accomplishment and encompasses mental, physical, social, and intellectual well-being. It is an invaluable and irreplaceable gift, unattainable through material means. Good health liberates individuals from the shackles of illness and bestows contentment and fulfillment in life.

(84) **Write an essay on**

Honesty is The Best Policy

The principle "honesty is the best policy" advocates for leading an upright life, which is fundamental for achieving success in both personal and professional spheres. It emphasizes that honesty is a cornerstone for trust in individuals, playing a crucial role in fostering a prosperous society and nation. When individuals and leaders are characterized by honesty, it reflects positively on the entire nation.

An honest individual navigates through situations with courage and confidence. Embracing honesty enables us to earn the trust of those around us, significantly impacting our relationships and various aspects of life. Honesty entails not only speaking the truth but also caring for and respecting the feelings of our associates. It involves demonstrating respect for everyone, regardless of their social status or abilities. An honest person refrains from passing judgment and treats all individuals with respect. This forms the foundation of their integrity.

Individuals who embody honesty are valued in personal relationships and business collaborations. Honesty manifests as a testament to a person's virtuous and honorable character, contributing to the development of exemplary traits. Honesty brings peace of mind, fostering satisfaction and creating a harmonious balance between body, mind, and spirit.

Honest individuals earn respect within families and society, while dishonest individuals often encounter challenges and negative perceptions from others. Honesty is vital for leading a prosperous life and is intertwined with developing good character. Thus, everyone must uphold honesty in their words and actions, as it forms the essence of a fulfilling life.

(85) **Write an essay on**

Save Earth

The Earth is a planet that is home to various species of animals, birds, reptiles, insects, etc. It is the only known planet in the universe with all the essential resources for life. As inhabitants of this planet, we are responsible for maintaining these resources to ensure a balanced environment. Famous slogans like "Save Earth, Save Environment" and "Save Earth, Save Life" aim to raise awareness about the importance of preserving our planet. This means keeping the Earth free from pollutants and ensuring it is suitable for all living beings. Unfortunately, the condition of our Earth is deteriorating due to pollution, deforestation, greenhouse gases, and more, negatively impacting the environment and the health of living beings.

Every year since 1970, the 22nd of April has been observed as Global Earth Day to promote environmental protection, although significant progress has yet to be seen. As the most intelligent species on Earth, it is crucial for us to keep the planet safe, clean, and habitable for all living beings, including plants and trees.

To protect the Earth, we should take the following measures:

1. Use water only when necessary, such as washing dirty clothes and using cold water.
2. Reduce greenhouse gas emissions by sharing private cars and public transport.
3. Use bicycles for local commuting.
4. Practice the 3R methods: reduce, reuse, and recycle.
5. Create compost as a natural fertilizer for crops instead of chemicals.
6. Use Compact Fluorescent Light bulbs (CFLs) to save energy.
7. Avoid unnecessary use of electric heaters or air conditioners.
8. Conserve electricity by switching off lights and fans and unplugging electric appliances.
9. Plant more trees to reduce pollution and the impact of greenhouse gases.

It's important to remember that we have not inherited the Earth; we are simply one species out of millions, and as intelligent beings, we are responsible for caring for the Earth for the sake of future generations.

(86) **Write an essay on**

Save Water

Water is an essential resource that sustains life on our planet, existing in various forms such as icebergs, snow, oceans, rivers, and underground sources. Despite its widespread presence, water scarcity remains a pressing issue globally. Only 3% of Earth's water is fresh and drinkable, making conserving this resource a universal responsibility for all living beings. Preserving water and trees is crucial, as both are fundamental to sustaining life and providing necessary oxygen and hydration.

The importance of water cannot be overstated; it is integral to the continuity of the life cycle on Earth. Water scarcity disproportionately affects different regions, with some areas facing severe challenges. For example, research by the United Nations has shown that girls in Rajasthan, India, cannot attend school due to the long distances they must travel to obtain water. This deprives them of an education and affects their overall development. Thus, water scarcity has far-reaching implications beyond access to water, impacting education and human development in these regions.

As responsible citizens, we must educate ourselves about water scarcity issues locally and globally. Through collective efforts, we can work towards water conservation, thus ensuring that a valuable resource is preserved for current and future generations. Every small action contributes to the more significant cause, like individual water droplets forming vast bodies of water such as ponds, rivers, and seas.

Simple adjustments to our daily habits can significantly improve water conservation. Practices such as turning off taps tightly after use and using a bucket and mug for washing and bathing instead of showers or pipes can collectively lead to substantial water savings. By making these positive changes in our daily activities, we can contribute to the "Save Water Campaign" and help alleviate water scarcity issues.

(87) **Write an essay on**

Swachh Bharat Abhiyan

The Swachh Bharat Mission, also known as the Swachh Bharat Abhiyan or Clean Bharat Mission, is a nationwide campaign initiated by the Government of Bharat on 2 October 2014. Its primary goals are eradicating open defecation, improving solid waste management, and creating Open Defecation-Free (ODF) villages.

The mission has two phases. Phase 1 of the Swachh Bharat Mission was implemented on 2 October 2019. Phase 2 aims to build upon the work done in the first phase and is planned in two periods: the first period was between 2020 and 21, and the second is ongoing until 2024–25. The initial target set for the mission was to achieve its goals by 2 October 2019, which marked the 150th anniversary of Mahatma Gandhi's birth.

The Bharatiya Government allocated about $28 billion (equivalent to Rs 2,29,600 crore) to achieve this. This funding resulted in an estimated 89.9 million toilet constructions (with subsidies provided to needy families between 2014 and 2019) in approximately 7,00,000 villages nationwide. Around 93% of the total funds were used for construction, while the remaining funds were allocated for behavior change campaigns and administration.

The mission was divided into rural and urban focuses. 'SBM - Gramin' for rural areas was overseen by the Ministry of Drinking Water and Sanitation (now under the Ministry of Jal Shakti), while 'SBM - urban' for urban areas was monitored by the Ministry of Housing and Urban Affairs.

However, the campaign received criticism for using coercive measures to compel people to use toilets. Some individuals were prevented from open defecation and were threatened with the withdrawal of government benefits. Despite these criticisms, Bharat achieved the status of being open-defecation-free in 2019, which contributed to fulfilling the Sustainable Development Goal (SDG) 6.2 health target ahead of the UN's target of 2030. The mission was launched to work towards the United Nations' Sustainable Development Goal Number 6, established in 2015.

(88) **Write an essay on**

Unity is Strength

Introduction:

The proverb- Unity is Strength emphasizes the importance of unity in every situation. Historical evidence and moral stories affirm that those united achieve the unachievable. Unity boosts morale and channels energies constructively.

Importance of Staying United:

Unity makes it easier to face and overcome difficulties and obstacles in life. Just as a family is important to us because it cherishes unity, trust, and love among family members in both challenging and happy times, friends, relatives, and good neighbors are valued for nourishing the concepts of unity and love. Unfortunately, these values are degrading quickly. We often fail to care for others and nourish love and respect for others, weakening the bonds of unity. Everything is interconnected. If you hate, others will hate you too. If you forget your duties, others will hardly care for you. It is time to move forward with positivity and leave all negativities behind. We should learn to give without expecting too much from others.

Conclusion:

"We are stronger if we are united, we are weak if we are divided" is a truth echoed by countless moral stories, history, and scriptures. We all know this truth but often choose to listen to our pride and self-esteem instead of our conscience. Finding faults in others should be abandoned to find ways to improve relations. This will help develop unity in families, societies, and nations. When all members feel the bond, a family, society, organization, or nation becomes more vigorous. Love and mutual respect are the foundation for being united. Selfishness, narrow-mindedness, and corrupted policies always spoil a good relationship and a sense of unity.

(89) **Write an essay on**

Work Is Worship

The famous proverb 'Work is Worship' emphasizes the idea that one cannot seek the blessings of God without putting in the effort. It highlights the responsibility placed on mankind, considered the most intelligent creation of God. The success and happiness of an individual is intricately intertwined with their hard work. Without exertion, one cannot attain anything. This is where the saying, 'An idle man's brain is the devil's workshop,' holds. Progress in science and numerous discoveries and inventions are all testament to humans' relentless hard work and patience. Consistent, focused effort in the right direction paves the way for a successful career and overall progression in life.
Integrating the concept of 'work is worship' into our individual lives is essential. The lives of great personalities worldwide exemplify the remarkable accomplishments resulting from their persistent hard work, driven by purpose, aim, or goal. Their dedication, tenacity, and intelligence have led to groundbreaking discoveries and creations that have not only changed the world but also earned them respect and admiration.
Hard work also significantly boosts self-confidence. While the effects may not be immediately apparent, the outcome is invariably an outstanding achievement, leading to a happy and fulfilling life. The development of prosperous nations such as the USA, Japan, China, and Germany is not a product of luck. It results from their citizens' collective, sustained efforts and hard work. A country's progression and growth are contingent upon the progress of its people.

9. ESSAYS on GENERAL TOPIC & EVENTS

(90) **Write an essay on**

Computer

The computer is one of the most important inventions of the 20th century. It has sped up activities and assists humans in various ways. It controls machines, helps in surgery, and is used in many fields. The computer is a beautiful and ingenious gift of science in the 21st century. It performs various tasks, from sewing to manufacturing cars and airplanes. Computers are easy to handle and take little time to learn and operate. Due to their ease of use and high work efficiency, they are used in numerous fields, such as offices, banks, hotels, educational institutions, shops, hospitals, commercial places, schools, colleges, training institutes, military establishments, military machines, industries, robot making, rocket launching, and space science.

Many people buy laptops or desktops for their kids to learn various things, from music to solving mathematics, and also for entertainment, like playing video games. With the help of the internet, computers serve as a large storage device and a comprehensive dictionary for saving various types of data such as information, study materials, projects, photos, images, videos, audio, songs, clips, games, and more. They are electronic machines capable of calculating and solving complex problems. They help enhance our skill levels and facilitate easy access to information. Computers are simple data-based machines that provide access to tools like paint tools, text tools, etc., which are highly beneficial for kids, children, and students to use more effectively.

We can use computers for accurate big or small mathematical calculations. They are used to provide weather forecasts, print books, publish newspapers, diagnose diseases, and much more. Computers are used for online railway reservations, ticket booking, and hotel or restaurant booking from anywhere worldwide. MNC companies use computers for accounting, invoicing, payroll, stock control, etc. It is now impossible to survive without a computer, and it will continue to be a great gift for future generations with new technologies.

(91) **Write an essay on**

Cricket

Cricket is one of India's most exciting outdoor games, and it is played in many countries worldwide. Indians are passionate about their love for cricket. During World Cup finals, the streets and government offices become empty as the frenzy of cricket fans celebrating victory is as evident as during Diwali.

It is a beautiful game played by two teams, each with 11 players. The game uses a bat and a ball in an open space and large stadiums. The games are pompously telecasted on TV, especially during national or international cricket competitions. Two players from one team start batting while the other team members do bowling and fielding. The team's captain, who wins the toss, decides whether their team will bat or bowl first. Generally, the team that wins the toss bats first, but the opposite can also occur. Alternatively, both teams can bat and bowl. The team that scores the most runs or takes the most wickets is declared the winner of the game.

There are many rules in cricket, and one cannot play cricket without knowing the laws and regulations properly. It is played best when the playing field is dry. Sachin Tendulkar was my favorite cricketer, and I enjoyed watching cricket games on TV during his time. Many talented cricketers are now playing the game, but I have not been following the sport as closely since then. Long live the game of cricket!

(92) **Write an essay on**

Disaster Management

Introduction: The vastness of the Bharatiya Territory requires safety measures beforehand. Bharat is a disaster-prone country, and disasters occur here frequently in many forms, including floods, hurricanes, earthquakes, tsunamis, landslides in hill areas, flash floods, epidemics, and some man-made disasters such as terrorist attacks, communal or political riots, breakdown of authority, and others.

As you can see, two major types of disasters have been stated above: natural and man-made. Both cause damage, loss of property, and human casualties. Disasters caused by natural reasons, which are beyond the control of human power, include floods, hurricanes, earthquakes, volcano eruptions, etc. These have immediate impacts on human lives. The man-made disasters are also known as complex emergencies. These are disasters caused by major accidents like fires, the breakdown of authority, looting, terrorist attacks, and political and religious riots.

Politics, which should guide a country, and religion, which should cause peace and prosperity in mind and society, are often misled and cause man-made disasters. I prefer not to go further into these details. However, for natural disasters that are beyond the control of human beings, a country or state government should take some precautions and safety measures beforehand to minimize the impact.

Disaster management is a continuous process of mitigating the impact of any disaster. It requires collective and coordinated efforts. Several activities need to be undertaken in the event of a disaster. The management includes coordination, command and control, rapid assessment of damage, restoration of power, telecommunication, well-equipped surface transport, deployment of search and rescue teams, sufficient medical and paramedical teams along with necessary equipment, arrangement for drinking water for the victims, food supplies, setting up of temporary shelters, sanitation and hygiene, identification and earmarking of resources, and maintenance of law and order, i.e., identifying the culprits or reasons behind, making arrests or taking necessary actions to improve the situation, etc.

Quick and timely response to any situation is the first condition of a sound disaster management system of a country or nation. A country's name and fame also depend on it. A sound disaster management system can save more human lives and reduce property damage. For this purpose, Bharat has set up many departments and organizations, such as the National Disaster Management Authority (NDMA), National Remote Sensing Centre (NRSC), Central Water Commission (CWC), etc.

Conclusion: Disaster management in any country has recently assumed great importance. Day after day, it advances with highly equipped, well-trained volunteers and officials and performs excellently in each country. It cannot avert the outbreak of disaster, particularly a natural one. Still, we can mitigate its impact to a large extent with the help of a sound disaster management system in any country or state.

(93) **Write an essay on**

Good Manners

Introduction:
Good manners refer to polite and positive social behavior, which is vital to maintaining smooth and positive relationships. Good manners help us win people's hearts in a crowd and give us a unique personality. They make us pleasant and obedient, genuinely loved and appreciated by all in society.

What are Good Manners:
Good manners are closely linked to moral rules. A person with good manners respects the feelings and sentiments of people around them. Modesty and courtesy are essential traits of a well-behaved person. Practicing good manners and following them throughout the day brings sunshine and adds qualities to life. It makes a person mentally happy and enriches their personality. Good manners should be instilled in children from a young age.

Teaching good manners to all students is beneficial to them and society. Talent and intelligence are not the only means to be a good person. Good manners make a person gentle and lovable and pave the way to a bright future. A lack of good manners and humanity among youths can lead them astray. As per the Law of Nature, intelligence and talent can take a wrong turn. Practicing good manners costs nothing but pays off throughout life. Some good manners include using magical words like "Sorry," "Thanks," "Please," and "Excuse me," which show readiness to accept mistakes, express gratitude, and more. These words should be used honestly, not as a tool to mock human sentiments and feelings.

Some good manners to learn include:
- Supporting people who are in pain and showing sympathy or empathy towards them
- Expressing politeness when dealing with people
- Being disciplined and punctual in daily life and activities
- Complimenting others for their excellent behavior and qualities
- Listening attentively to people who are talking to us
- Asking for permission before using someone else's things
- Responding with a smile to others' questions
- Not interrupting during meetings of elders and waiting for our turn
- Showing respect to elders, parents, and teachers
- Knocking on the door before entering someone else's bedroom or office

Conclusion:
Practicing good manners costs nothing but gives much more throughout your life. People with polite and pleasant natures are always admired and exert magnetic influence over others. Therefore, we must practice and follow good manners in our lives and daily activities.

Based on the above, You can write a paragraph on **'the Necessity of Good Manners.'**

(94) **Write an essay on**

Happiness

Happiness is a state of bliss. If you train your brain to stay in this state, it will remain this way because your mind believes whatever you say. However, it is not as simple as it seems. You may experience happiness occasionally; however, it may take months or even years to make this state last.

Ways to Attract Happiness and Make it Last: According to recent studies, some of the habits to attract happiness and make it last are as follows:

1. Be Content: Instead of getting super excited or depressed in different situations, you must practice transforming these activated feelings into deactivated feelings, such as calmness and contentment. These feelings are healthier and more accessible to sustain. Practice sustaining them even in bad times.

2. **Live in the Present:** Stop thinking about your past mistakes. Everyone makes mistakes; nobody is perfect. Stop blaming yourself or feeling guilty for all the wrong decisions you may have made. Also, stop worrying about your future. Live in the present moment. Don't let the good times go unnoticed. What will come, will come – why worry beforehand?

3. Be Thankful: Remember all your past moments and decisions that brought happiness and made you rejoice. Be thankful to God or to the people who bestowed such joyous moments.

4. Develop Positive Thoughts: Your thoughts build your reality. Positive thoughts and a positive mind attract positive things that lead to happiness; negative thoughts bring similar experiences and make you unhappy. So, the only way to experience joy is to feel good about everything you have.

5. Surround Yourself with Positive People: Avoid people who indulge in negative talk or demotivate you. Surround yourself with positive minds instead.

Conclusion: It is easy to get carried away by negative thoughts and become anxious and stressed due to several things in life. To stay with positive thoughts and energy, people need continuous practice. The rest is your choice—you want to lead a life of happiness or a life full of anxiety and loneliness.

(95) **Write an essay on**

Human Rights

The Universal Declaration of Human Rights was adopted by the UN in 1948. It is a seminal document that aims to safeguard people's natural rights to live and thrive. Human rights can be categorized into natural rights and civil rights. Civil rights are protected by a nation's laws based on human beings' natural rights.

Human rights are fundamental norms delineating specific standards of human behavior, ensuring that individuals can live and prosper. They are inherent to every individual simply because they are human. Some fundamental human rights include the right to life, fair trial, freedom of thought, conscience, and religion, freedom from slavery, and freedom from torture.

Additionally, universal human rights encompass rights such as liberty, personal and social security, freedom of speech, access to education, right to own property, the right to marriage and family, freedom of movement, and freedom from discrimination. The United Nations Human Rights Council, along with National Human Rights Commissions in various countries, upholds these rights and takes necessary measures to protect the human rights of global citizens and address any violations.

(96) **Write an essay on**

Importance of Healthy Food

Introduction: Have you ever wondered why your parents and teachers insist on eating healthy food? "Healthy food is one of the most important parts of leading a healthy life, and the other is regular exercise."

The cause of obesity and its remedy: The rate of obesity (overweightness) has increased from 4% in the 1970s to a staggering 18% in 2010 and is continuing to rise. One of the key factors contributing to this trend is bad food habits and the increasing fascination with Junk Food. Being overweight or obese can put children, as well as adults, at a higher risk of health problems such as heart disease, hypertension, diabetes, and more.

The famous proverb **"Health is wealth"** reminds us of the importance of good health. We should always strive to have a balanced diet that includes more vegetables and fruits daily, as vegetables can provide vital nutrients for good health. Consuming vegetables and fruits regularly helps keep our bodies fit and healthy. While we may be busy daily, we should never skip breakfast and ideally have a light dinner. Young boys and girls are easily fascinated by the world of burgers, chips, fried chicken, and soft drinks, and so are adults. These foods are now correctly described as 'Junk,' meaning 'useless' or 'of little value.' We should avoid these foods and engage in regular physical exercise to stay healthy.

Concluding statement: In recent years, a growing trend towards vegetarianism has arisen among young people due to their increasing awareness of health, concern for the environment, and compassion for animals. This is a good sign. We should encourage our children to avoid junk food and embrace a healthy lifestyle.

(97) **Write an essay on**

INTERNET

Introduction: Modern life has become much easier, thanks to the significant contributions of science, technology, and the Internet.

Meaning of the word 'INTERNET': The internet is the global system of interconnected computer networks, also known as 'Interconnected Networks' of computers. 'INTERNET' refers to regional or local networks and the global network system of interconnected computers, servers, phones, and smart appliances. It uses the Transmission Control Protocol (TCP) standard to exchange information and files quickly. Sometimes, the INTERNET is also referred to as "NET." The internet is now an indispensable part of people's everyday lives worldwide.

Popular internet services include:
- Email
- VoIP (Voice over IP)
- SMS (Short Message Service)

Use and abuse of the Internet: The Internet allows us to access the World Wide Web from any location, providing various facilities such as e-mail, search engines, web portals, informative websites, software updates, video chatting, calling, and sending and receiving messages. Internet availability is very beneficial for students and individuals seeking efficient learning methods.

However, along with its benefits, the Internet has disadvantages. It can be a big concern, especially for students, as objectionable and improper materials are easily accessible. Parents are often helpless in controlling their children's internet usage. Teaching young kids how to use computers and the Internet is essential but not always practical. Internet usage is prohibited in some countries, like North Korea and Myanmar.

Concluding Lines: Despite the potential for misuse, such as internet hackers stealing private information without one's knowledge, we cannot overlook the internet's importance and essentiality in the present global scenario.

(98) **Write an essay on**

Junk Food

The term "junk food" clearly indicates its detrimental effects on health. Though it means "useless" or "of little value," junk food poses a serious threat to health due to its high calorie, fat, cholesterol, sugar, and salt content. Nowadays, kids and teenagers are more inclined to consume junk foods, perhaps due to their appealing flavors. However, regular or excessive consumption of junk food leads to various health issues. This often results in frequent visits to doctors, medical tests, and the need for medication. Common junk foods such as chips, fries, snacks, burgers, pizzas, and pasta offer little to no nutritional value and can negatively impact health, such as weight gain and various health problems.

The high-calorie content of junk foods can lead to exhaustion and lack of energy due to the absence of essential nutrients. Additionally, consumption of junk food can result in frequent food cravings, delivery of unhealthy fats, and poor brain function. Excessive consumption of junk foods can also lead to high cholesterol levels, plaque formation in the arteries, heart problems, liver damage, weight gain, and an increased risk of developing conditions such as diabetes and high blood pressure, particularly in children.

In conclusion, parents must teach their kids healthy eating habits early to avoid the detrimental effects of junk food on their health.

(99) **Write an essay on**

Nature

Introduction: Nature is an essential and integral part of everyone's lives. It is God's beautiful creation and a precious gift to us. We should never miss the pleasure of enjoying the nature that surrounds us. Nature has been a favorite topic of works by countless famous poets, writers, painters, and artists from different regions and countries.

What is Nature/The Form of Nature: Nature includes everything that surrounds us, such as water, air, land, sky, fire, rivers, forests, animals, birds, plants, sun, moon, stars, sea, lake, rain, thunder, storm, etc. Nature comes in different colors, forms, and shapes and includes living and non-living things. Everything, including all human beings, is a part of nature, and each part has its power, importance, or significance provided by God. God is the ultimate power and the source of all energy, expressed in the form of Nature, which is worshiped differently in different religions.

The Influence of Nature: Nature has a mighty transformative power that changes our mood and behavior accordingly. We feel happy and hopeful in the sunshine. The rainy and spring seasons give specific people hope for nature's productivity and harvest time. People feel so glad in the moonlight, poets get inspiration, and we may feel bored and tired in bright sunlight. Nature has healing, destructive, and creative power and can significantly impact us. A patient may recover sooner if provided with a suitable and pleasant environment.

Conclusion: As responsible beings, we should keep our environment and nature clean and preserve them for future generations. Maintaining the proper balance of all elements in nature is essential to sustain life on Earth. Our awareness and actions may allow us to peacefully exist on Earth for millions of years or face annihilation due to Earth's destructive forces if we don't take care of nature.

(100) **Write an essay on**

Pollution

Introduction: Pollution is the contamination introduced into the natural environment, causing adverse changes to nature and the environment. This contamination may occur in smoke, dust, sewage, and unbearable noise.

Pollution Today and Its Causes: Pollution has become a serious issue as people face many health hazards daily. Various types of pollutants from industrial waste and other activities are contaminating our natural resources, such as air, water, and soil. Pollution rates in cities are higher than in villages due to the large number of vehicles, with fumes from vehicles and factories causing air pollution that is unfit for breathing. Sewage, household garbage, and industrial by-products directly mix into rivers, lakes, and oceans, causing water pollution. Solid waste, garbage, plastic, and other unused items thrown on land are causing soil pollution and affecting crop production. Noise pollution from celebrations and events also affects public health, leading to problems like deafness.

Concluding Lines: The quality of life is worsening as pollution causes various health ailments such as high blood pressure, kidney disorders, respiratory diseases, cancer, epidemics, and skin diseases. It is essential to control pollution before it destroys us.

(101) **Read the features given about a season of the year. Identify the season and write a paragraph on it.**

(Features: Summer season—scorching sun—too heat—people sweat—feel thirsty—need fans, AC, Cooler—occasional black clouds floating and thunderstorms—mangoes, jackfruits, litchis—roses, hibiscus, sunflower, aparajita (clitoria)—why you like it.**)**

Summer Season

"The summer season brings intense heat and scorching sun, causing people to sweat profusely and feel incredibly thirsty. We rely on fans, air conditioners, and coolers to find relief to temper the heat. Occasionally, black clouds float in the sky, heralding thunderstorms that offer moments of respite. The season also brings a delightful array of fruits, such as mangoes, jackfruits, and litchis, adding a tropical touch to the atmosphere. Vibrant blooms like roses, hibiscus, sunflowers, and aparajita (clitoria) further enrich the visual landscape. Despite the challenges, the unique combination of elements during summer has its undeniable appeal. What draws you to this season?"

(102) **Write an essay on**

Rainy Season

The rainy season is a lovely time for everyone. It typically begins in July and ends in September, following the hot summer season. The rain rejuvenates living things that have dried up due to the summer heat, offering new hope and life.

During this time, nature receives much-needed relief from the cool rainwater. Ponds, rivers, and streams that have dried up during the hot summer become replenished. The rainy season breathes new life into water animals and provides water for farmers, allowing for the cultivation of crops. The return of greenery to gardens and lawns transforms the environment, giving it an appealing new look.

Despite its short duration of only three months, the rainy season holds excellent significance for farmers, especially in India, who rely on abundant water for their crops. Many farmers construct pits and ponds to collect rainwater throughout the year, making the rainy season a valuable boon.

The season also adds to the scenic beauty of the environment and holds economic benefits for farmers. Seeing lush greenery and running clouds in the sky delight painters and nature lovers. I love the greenery and the sight of running clouds over the sky during the rainy season. I often venture outside with my friends to relish each moment, from the gentle showers and falling drops of water from trees to the thrilling experience of birds bathing and taking shelter from sudden lightning strikes.

Last year, I visited Nainital with my parents and had some fantastic experiences. It was a unique experience to feel watery clouds touching our bodies as we drove through the area, with some clouds even entering through the car window. The slow, gentle rain was thoroughly enjoyable, and we even went water boating in Nainital, surrounded by lush greenery.

(103) **Read the features given about a season of the year. Identify the season and write a paragraph on it.**

(Features: Winter Season--cold wind, mist in the morning—pleasant sunshine during daytime—cold weather—wear woolen clothes, use blankets or quilts—dahlias, marigolds—oranges, grapes—suitable time for picnics—people in tropical and sub-tropical areas like it much.**)**

Winter Season

Sample 1

During the winter, you can expect cold winds and mist in the morning but pleasant sunshine. It's cold, so wearing woolen clothes and using blankets or quilts is advisable. You'll find dahlias, marigolds blooming, oranges and grapes. It's a suitable time for picnics, and people in tropical and sub-tropical areas particularly enjoy this season. (62 words)

Sample 2

Winter brings a chilly atmosphere characterized by cold winds and misty mornings. However, once the day progresses, the sun brings a pleasant warmth. The cold weather necessitates woolen clothes and cozy blankets or quilts. This season is marked by the blooming of dahlias and marigolds and an abundance of oranges and grapes. It's a perfect time for picnics, and individuals residing in tropical and sub-tropical regions eagerly anticipate and thoroughly enjoy this time of the year. (83 words)

Sample 3

Winter is the coldest season of the year. It is one of the most favorite seasons in tropical and sub-tropical countries. It comes after late autumn and before the spring season. Mist and a cold breeze are blowing in the morning. However, during the daytime, the sun shines pleasantly. People wear warm or woolen clothes and use blankets or quilts at night as the weather remains cold or freezing. Dahlias, marigolds, etc., are seasonal flowers, and oranges and grapes have become available in the market. Winter is the best season for outdoor picnics. Being an inhabitant of a sub-tropical area, winter is my favorite season. (106)

The Spring Season

(104) Write a paragraph in 100 words on the changes that you may have noticed in nature when the Spring Season comes after Winter:

Spring Awakening

When spring arrives after winter, nature undergoes a magnificent change. The once-empty and dull scenery becomes alive with new colors and life. Trees start growing tiny buds that eventually turn into beautiful flowers. The air becomes fragrant with the sweet scent of blooming blossoms. Once barren fields become covered in lush green grass and colorful blossoms. The sound of birds singing fills the air as they return from their winter migration. The days become longer, the sun shines brighter, and everything feels fresh and renewed. It's a magical time that shows us how nature renews itself and reminds us of the beauty of life's cycles.

(105) **Write a paragraph within 100 words on the water cycle, using the flow-chart:**

(Water evaporates from water bodies, rising as vapor, getting heavier, condensing, forming clouds, and falling to earth as rain.)

Water Cycle

The water cycle is one of the most fascinating natural phenomena in the universe, essential for supporting life on Earth. It goes through several stages. During the day, the heat from the sun causes water bodies to become warm, leading to increased evaporation. Winds then carry this water vapor throughout the day and night. As the vapor rises into the upper atmosphere, it condenses and mixes with dust, smoke, and other particles to form clouds that float in the sky. When these clouds pass through a cold region or experience a drop in temperature, the condensed water becomes heavier and falls back to Earth as rain. This cycle then repeats itself continuously.

(106) **Write an essay on**

Road Safety

Human resources are always considered precious for society, the economy, and the nation. A secured life is an asset to the person and his nation. To give a secure life, every nation has set some rules and regulations for its citizens, which we should follow honestly and sincerely for the benefit of ourselves and also for the nation. Some of these rules are the road safety rules or Traffic signals. Please read the following:

Safety Rules:
- Traffic light signals should be followed sincerely.
- The speed limit of bikes, cars, buses, and trucks should be maintained.
- We should not listen to music or talk over mobile phones when driving.

How to cross the road

- Hold your mother's or your dad's hand tight. If you are an adult or a big boy, just be careful while crossing the road. Remember, that is not your house lawn.

- Find a safe place (zebra cross, if any) to cross the road.

- Stop at the road sign. Study, also the other signs and know their meanings.

- Think carefully before leap.

- Look left.

- Look right and all around you.

- Listen to the horns of the cars if anyone is coming.

- Then cross the road safely and remember these for all the time.

Often, road accidents take place that take lives too; it is due to the rules being compromised. They are not strictly followed by men. Lives will be secured when people sincerely follow them while traveling on the roads. Everyone should respect others while driving or walking on the road and ensure their safety. Traffic signals are one of the most essential aspects of Road safety rules to secure our lives and avoid roadside accidents, injuries, and deaths. Other measures that can be included in the list are essential awareness about the vehicle's speed, defensive driving according to weather and road conditions, the proper use of vehicle lights and horn, wearing seat belts, wearing helmets, the proper use of vehicle mirrors, avoiding over-speeding, understanding road lights, maintaining a safe distance of the vehicle on the road, proper understanding of handling crises, and following awareness telecasts and documentaries on TV, etc.

However, some people, such as those blind from birth, hardly care about all these precautions and safety measures and cause injuries or deaths of others, including themselves. Some drive recklessly, some cross as if it is their house lawn, and some are too busy talking over their phones while driving or crossing a road. Some hardly notice traffic signals; some are too arrogant of their positions or power. All these merely cause frequent road accidents. Strict laws are suitable for all of them.

(107) **Write an essay on**

Sports

Sports and good education are the keys to a child's success in life. Sports and games promote physical and mental fitness and offer many hidden benefits. Sports help develop concentration among students. A famous saying goes, "Sports gives a sound mind in a sound body." This means having a well-functioning mind in a fit body is essential for success.

Regularly playing sports boosts confidence and teaches discipline, which remains with us throughout our lives. Encouraging children to be involved in sports and cultivating their interest in games is essential. Many types of sports are named according to their rules and ways of playing. Some examples of sports include cricket, hockey, football, basketball, volleyball, tennis, running, skipping, high and low jumping, discus throw, badminton, rowing, swimming, kho-kho, and kabaddi.

Some sports are played outdoors on open grounds, while others are indoor games played within a confined space. Sports help individuals deal with life's ups and downs, balancing body and mind, excitement and sorrow. In schools, playing sports for some hours daily is considered necessary for children's well-being and the country's future. Sports are incorporated into the curriculum, and good athletes are recognized based on their performance in co-curricular activities. For professional athletes, training in specialized institutions or centers under the guidance of suitable coaches is essential.

(108) **Write an essay on**

Value of Time

"There is a common and true saying that 'Time and Tide waits for none,' which means time never waits for anyone. One should have to go with time and use the time properly. Time costs us a lot; once it goes, it never comes back or returns. It never stays for anyone. It is unbounded, which means no one can limit time within a boundary. Time makes everyone dance around. Nothing in this world can defeat it or win from it. Time is the most robust instrument in the world, which can damage and improve anyone, from a little creature to a planet. The whole universe is in the grip of Time. Nothing is beyond it.

Time is very powerful; one can kneel before it but never defeat it or snatch victory from it. We cannot measure its potential because sometimes only one moment is enough to win, while other times it takes a whole life to win. Only one moment is enough to create a difference between life and death. Every moment brings lots of golden opportunities to us; we need to understand and use the indication of time. It is favorable for those who appreciate its value and use it correctly; however, it is unfavorable for the idle people who waste it or misuse it.

Every moment is an enormous storehouse of new chances in life. So, we should never let go of such precious time; instead, make full use of it. We should never allow our golden time to pass away from us unnecessarily. We should utilize time positively and fruitfully to reach our destination. The best way to utilize time helpfully is to make a timetable to do everything correctly and try to do things on time."

(109) **Write an essay on**

Yoga

Yoga is an essential and precious gift passed down by our ancestors. It connects with nature, uniting the mind and body to achieve perfect harmony. Through yoga, one can attain higher consciousness and control over the body in every aspect - physically, mentally, socially, and intellectually. In schools and colleges, yoga is encouraged daily to benefit students and enhance their concentration levels. It is a systematic effort to attain perfection by gaining control over the natural elements within the body.

Regular and safe yoga practice is essential to benefit from all its asanas. Yoga aims to progress spiritually and develop self-development by controlling inner energy. Central to yoga is the process of inhaling and exhaling, which is paramount. Daily yoga practice prevents illness and can even cure various diseases, including serious ones such as cancer, diabetes, high/low blood pressure, heart and kidney disorders, liver disorders, gynecological issues, and various mental problems.

In the present day, practicing yoga is crucial for improving our lives, but there are obstacles from religious perspectives. Some communities or individuals oppose it due to their religious beliefs, even in the 21st century. Despite this, daily yoga strengthens the inner and outer body and boosts the immune system. As an alternative system of medicine, it can reduce the side effects of heavy medications. The best time to practice yoga is early morning, providing a conducive environment to gain control over the body and mind quickly. Lastly, yoga purifies the heart, brain, and mind.

10. ESSAYS on OCCASIONS & CELEBRATIONS

(110) **Write an essay on**

Children's Day

Introduction: 'Children's Day' in India is celebrated every year on the birth anniversary of Pandit Jawaharlal Nehru. It aims to focus on and improve the status of children in the country, as they are future citizens. Children's Day has been celebrated in India since 1956 on November 14th.

Reason for Celebrating Children's Day: A happy childhood ensures a confident and positive adult who is expected to be a responsible citizen of the country. The goal of the occasion is connected to various government incentive schemes aimed at providing a healthy and fulfilling life to every child in the country. The day emphasizes ensuring a healthy life for children and addressing children's issues to benefit society and the nation. Brave children are honored with prizes and certificates to encourage them to become responsible citizens of the country in the future. In addition, various child incentive schemes and scholarships for children from different backgrounds are launched or renewed every year on this particular day.

Observance of Children's Day: Many competitions are organized at school and primary levels to observe children's development. Prizes, awards, certificates, and incentives are distributed among the children, with some receiving scholarships. Observing the Day aims to give children opportunities to showcase their talents and abilities. Additionally, the day draws attention to children's issues and highlights their importance to the authorities and the government every year.

Conclusion: Children's Day is celebrated to raise awareness that children are the country's real future. Responsible citizens, parents, and elder siblings have a joint duty to guide and support all children, at least those in their vicinity, to help them prosper, provide them with proper education, and discourage child labor so that they can become dutiful citizens shortly and successful contributors to the nation.

(111) **Write an essay on**

Christmas

Christmas falls every winter, and people celebrate it with lots of joy, activities, and happiness. It is one of the most important festivals for Christians, and they celebrate it with lots of preparation. The preparation for the celebration starts a month before and ends 12 days after Christmas. Christmas is celebrated worldwide, not only by Christians but also by people of other religions, lovingly and festively. It is held on December 25th, and the entire celebration revolves around this date.

Christmas is celebrated on the birth anniversary of the Lord Jesus Christ, who founded Christianity. Today, people decorate a Christmas tree and invite their friends, relatives, and neighbors to enjoy and exchange gifts. Santa Claus comes with gifts for all children, bringing them immense joy. Schools, colleges, universities, offices, and other government and non-government organizations are closed on December 25th, making it a universal holiday enjoyed by Christians and non-Christians worldwide.

This festive occasion brings families together, allowing all members to come together and share lots of fun. It is an opportunity for unity, with people preparing delicious dishes, sweets, fruits, and nuts for the dining table. Everyone wears colorful clothes, dances, sings, attends parties, and participates in adventurous activities. Today, Christians offer prayers, confess their sins and sufferings, sing holy songs, seek forgiveness for the original sin, and share their love and care with friends, relatives, and loved ones.

(112) **Write an essay on**

Dussehra

The celebration of Dussehra signifies the victory of Lord Rama over the demon king Ravana. Lord Rama represents truth, while Ravana symbolizes evil power. This festival lasts ten days, with the first nine days dedicated to worshipping the goddess Durga and the tenth day, Vijay Dashami when people celebrate Lord Rama's victory over Ravana. Dussehra is a major festival in the Hindu religion and is celebrated throughout the country. It falls every year in September or October, twenty days before the Diwali festival. Hindus celebrate this festival with great religious fervor, including worshipping goddess Durga.

The traditions and customs associated with this festival vary from region to region. The preparations for the festival start a few days before the exact date. Large fairs are organized for ten days or even a month in some places, attracting people from distant regions who come to shop at temporary shops or stalls set up on public grounds. In cities and towns, permanent stalls provide a wide range of items for public purchase, from cosmetics to electric vehicles. In many parts of the country, dramatic shows depicting Dussehra's legends are arranged daily.

Paper models of Ravan, Kumbhkarn, and Meghnath are set up in the Ram Lila ground, and various significant events from the life of Lord Rama are acted out by individuals who play the roles of Rama, Sita, and Lakshman. Every year, thousands of men, women, and children from nearby regions come to enjoy these performances.

(113) **Write an essay on**

Holiday

A student's life mainly consists of homework, exam preparation, and tests, leaving little room for anything else. That's why holidays are so important—they break up the monotony of constant studying. This need for a break isn't exclusive to students. It applies to employees, workers, business people, and even stay-at-home parents. Doing the same work daily can lead to boredom and a decline in productivity due to a lack of innovation. We all need a break. We need holidays.

For students, weekends provide a brief respite, and there are longer holidays throughout the year. For others, planning is required. Vacations offer the opportunity to recharge, relax, and return to work or studies refreshed and full of energy. Different regions and countries have varying reasons for extended vacations, such as weather or festivals. For example, in West Bengal, there are Summer and Puja vacations, and countries in cold regions often have two months of Winter vacation.

While some students attend special classes or courses during long vacations, many enjoy their time off by taking trips and pursuing their hobbies. Holidays play an essential role in everyone's life. I eagerly look forward to my annual family trips after the end of each holiday. It's a time for me to unwind and enjoy life.

Holidays allow us to step away from our regular routines, engage in our hobbies, reconnect with old friends, and spend time with extended family members. However, it's also essential to not neglect our studies, even during holidays.

(114) **Write an essay on**

Importance of Holidays

We all love holidays. From school-going kids to working employees, everyone looks forward to holidays. Everyone must rest and refresh their daily routine. When we get tired and bored with our regular routine, holidays come like refreshing showers that relax our tired bodies and minds.

Holidays are important because they allow us to rest and enjoy ourselves with our friends and family. A single holiday can change our routine and provide more relaxation from day-to-day activities.

As citizens of a tropical country, we all look forward to summer vacation, or, being Bengali, we eagerly wait for our puja vacation. A long vacation period allows us to tour outside of our homeland or visit our dearest relatives, cousins, and grandparents and spend the most pleasing time with them.

When continuous work and study affect our health and minds and produce boredom, holidays come as a blessing to refresh us. They reduce stress, give us rest from daily work, and rejuvenate us. After the break, one can work with new enthusiasm. That's why everyone, from students to employees or businessmen, waits for and welcomes it. Indeed, a holiday is necessary for anyone who wants to rest from their daily routine.

(115) **Write an essay on**

Independence Day

Independence is a universal desire shared by all people and creatures. In the context of "Independence Day," it signifies explicitly freedom from foreign rule. India gained its independence from British colonial rule on August 15, 1947. In 2022, India celebrated its 75th Independence Day anniversary, marking its journey as a growing global power with aspirations for further development.

India, with its rich heritage and ancient roots, enthusiastically observes Independence Day. August 15 is officially designated as a National Festival Day and a national holiday. The day is marked by cultural programs and performances in schools, colleges, banks, and offices nationwide.

On Independence Day, Indians pay homage to the leaders and freedom fighters who sacrificed their lives for the nation's independence. The day is filled with various activities, including parades, patriotic song performances, and gatherings with family and friends. Prime Minister hoists the tricolor National Flag at the Red Fort in Delhi, followed by a speech and other events such as parades and gun salutes.
Independence Day reminds us of India's glorious past and encourages citizens to take pride in their culture and heritage. It is also an occasion to pledge respect for other cultures, religions, customs, and national identities, embracing cooperation and coexistence over isolation.

(116) **Your school celebrated Sports Day on 20th February**. The famous cricketer Rohit Sharma was the Chief Guest for the occasion. Write a description of the event in 100-150 words.

Sports Day Celebration at School

This year, our school celebrated Sports Day on 20th February. The famous cricketer Rohit Sharma was the Chief Guest on the occasion. The Sports Day started with a march past by the school students in white and blue uniforms, with national and our school flags in hand. It was a unique sight with the sounds and cheers of the boys all around the playground, and the program for the day was inaugurated with the flag hoisting by our honorable headmaster. The guests and others were honored with flowers, and a brief cultural program was performed. We felt honored in the presence of our chief guest this year, Mr. Rohit Sharma, the international cricket player. He shared wisdom: "Dedication and hard work is the cornerstone for success." He encouraged the youngsters to incorporate sports into their lifestyle, as playing a game develops many qualities like team spirit, cooperation, and friendship in individuals, and helps to stay fit and healthy. His presence at the program made it one of the most memorable days in our lives.

(117) **Write an essay on**

Summer Vacation

Vacation is always a period that every student looks forward to. It allows us to indulge in our favorite hobbies. Summer vacation is particularly delightful, as it offers a lot. It is the season for enjoying fruits like mangoes, jackfruits, and litchis in India, which are favorites among many people. It's also the perfect time for trips and exploring new places. I often go on tours with my parents and brother. During the last trip, we visited Ooty. Since summer vacation is relatively long, students can dedicate time to improving skills and knowledge in subjects they may lack. Additionally, it provides a chance to visit relatives and loved ones and reconnect with our roots by visiting our native place, especially if it's far from our current residence. Many people also take the opportunity to spend time with their grandparents. I particularly enjoy spending quality time with my grandma and savoring the fresh vegetables and fruits she grows in her fields. Therefore, summer vacation brings joy to young children like my brother and me. We eagerly anticipate this time after spending days engaged in rigorous work and studies.

(118) **Write an essay on**

Teachers' Day

Dr. Sarvepalli Radhakrishnan (5 September 1888 – 17 April 1975) was a passionate advocate of education and renowned as a scholar, philosopher, diplomat, and teacher. He served as the 1st Vice President of India from 1952 to 1962 and the 2nd President of India from 1962 to 1967. In honor of his contributions, his birthday, September 5th, has been celebrated as Teachers' Day in India since 1962 to honor Dr. Sarvepalli Radhakrishnan and all teachers for their unique contributions to society and for nurturing future citizens.

Dr. Sarvepalli Radhakrishnan held a deep affection for the teaching profession. He advocated for the advancement of teachers in the country and encouraged higher education among them. Every year, the Government of India honors select teachers for their contributions to the field of education on September 5th. Additionally, in each institution, all teachers are honored with gifts, flowers, and respect from their students. Some interested students are allowed to take charge of classes for the day, perhaps to inspire them to pursue teaching in the future. The significance of Teacher's Day lies in fostering a healthy relationship and understanding between teachers and students, which is particularly important in today's scenario, where political influences can disrupt the teacher-student dynamic in colleges and universities.

Teaching is a profession that can shape the future. It is unfortunate when teachers and students forget their ideals and duties to the institution and instead act based on political motives, tarnishing its essence. The same sentiment applies to World Teachers' Day, celebrated on October 5th each year, and I would like to pay tribute to all teachers worldwide.

(119) International Women's Day is celebrated worldwide with great enthusiasm. As part of the celebrations, the Rotary Club of your city awarded women achievers. Among those honored included the famous Police Officer

Arpita Paul, a singer Monali Tagore, and Shilpa, a social worker in the town. Write a short description of this event for your school magazine.

The International Women's Day Celebration

On March 8th, we annually observe International Women's Day to celebrate the achievements and contributions of women in our community and society as a whole. It's a day to acknowledge their impact on their families and the nation. Each year, the Rotary Club in our city hosts a special event to honor outstanding women from our town. This year's event recognized several successful women, including Police Officer Arpita Paul, the talented singer Monali Tagore, and the dedicated social worker Shilpa, who have made significant strides in their respective fields.

During the event, Ms. Arpita Paul shared an inspiring message with the young girls in the city, urging them to be vigilant against social challenges and promising to support them when needed. Ms. Tagore emphasized the importance of education, encouraging girls to pursue their studies to build confidence. She also delighted the audience with two heartfelt songs. Shilpa underscored the significance of promoting education and raising awareness among all members of society. All these remarkable women reaffirmed their commitment to working towards women's empowerment in our country.

The celebration also featured children's creative contributions, showcasing their remarkable drawings depicting influential women from various fields, including Sister Nivedita, Mother Teresa, Sunita Williams, Kalpana Chawla, Mithali Raj, Mary Kom, and Sirisha Bandla. These drawings amplified the message of gender equality and female empowerment.

The program began at 5 p.m. and concluded around 9 p.m. at the city auditorium, concluding an inspiring and memorable observance of International Women's Day.

(120) **Try to write a paragraph on each of the following:**

Earthquake

An earthquake is a natural disaster caused by the abrupt release of energy in the Earth's crust that creates seismic waves. These waves can cause the ground to shake and result in the destruction of buildings and infrastructure and loss of lives. Earthquakes can vary in size and intensity, and they are often followed by aftershocks, more minor tremors that occur after the main shock. Regions located near tectonic plate boundaries are more susceptible to earthquakes. Communities need to have emergency preparedness plans in place to minimize the impact of earthquakes and ensure the safety of residents.

Value of discipline

The value of discipline in students' lives cannot be overstated. Discipline is essential for academic success and personal development. It instills important virtues such as punctuality, responsibility, and self-control. Students who cultivate discipline can better manage their time effectively, stay organized, and remain focused on their goals. This leads to better academic performance and prepares students for the challenges they will face in their future careers. Moreover, discipline helps students develop a strong work ethic and the resilience to overcome obstacles. Overall, instilling discipline in students' lives fosters a sense of accountability and sets the foundation for their academic and professional success.

Science: it uses and abuses (an essay)

Science, the systematic study of the structure and behavior of the physical and natural world through observation and experiment, has undeniably changed the course of human history and revolutionized how we live. It has provided us with countless innovations and discoveries that have improved our quality of life, expanded our understanding of the universe, and facilitated incredible advancements in various fields. However, like any powerful tool, science can be subject to misuse and exploitation, leading to potentially harmful consequences.

The uses of science are plentiful and far-reaching. It has contributed to significant improvements in medicine, allowing for the development of life-saving drugs, treatments, and surgical procedures. Moreover, scientific research and technological advancements have enhanced our understanding of complex diseases and paved the way for breakthroughs in healthcare. In addition, science has fueled progress in agriculture, leading to increased crop yields, disease resistance in plants, and the development of sustainable farming practices. Furthermore, technological innovations from scientific research have transformed communication, transportation, and manufacturing, making these processes more efficient and accessible.

Despite its myriad benefits, science can also be subject to abuses. One prominent example is the environmental impact of specific scientific and technological practices. The uncontrolled exploitation of natural resources and the release of pollutants have led to ecological degradation and climate change. Additionally, weaponry and military technology advancements have raised concerns about the proliferation of destructive weaponry and the potential for global conflict. Furthermore, ethical issues arise in fields such as genetic engineering, where the manipulation of gene material raises questions about the boundaries of scientific intervention and potential long-term consequences.

To mitigate the abuses of science, it is essential to emphasize responsible scientific practices, ethical guidelines, and the regulation of potentially harmful technologies. Education and public awareness regarding the ethical implications of scientific developments are crucial in ensuring that the potential negative consequences of scientific progress are minimized. Additionally, fostering interdisciplinary collaboration and ethical decision-making within the scientific community is vital in preventing the misuse of scientific knowledge and technologies.

In conclusion, science is a powerful force for positive change and progress in society, providing countless benefits and advancements that have improved the human condition. Its impact on various aspects of human life is undeniable, and its potential for further positive developments is vast. However, it is imperative to acknowledge and address the potential abuses of science, ensuring that ethical considerations and responsible practices are incorporated into scientific endeavors to safeguard against harmful outcomes. By recognizing the dual nature of science and promoting its responsible use, we can harness its potential for the greater good while minimizing its potential for harm.

Visit to an Exhibition last winter

Last winter, I had the opportunity to visit a fascinating science exhibition that captivated my imagination. The exhibition showcased diverse, innovative scientific concepts, interactive displays, and hands-on experiments that left a lasting impression on me. I was particularly intrigued by the demonstrations of cutting-edge technology, environmental sustainability solutions, and breakthroughs in medical research. The engaging presentations and informative discussions with scientists and researchers expanded my understanding of various scientific fields. Overall, the experience was enlightening and inspiring, reinforcing my appreciation for the extraordinary scientific advancements. (85 words)

Need for moral education in school

Value education in schools plays a crucial role in shaping the character and morality of students. It goes beyond academic knowledge, teaching students important life lessons such as honesty, respect, empathy, and responsibility. By integrating value education into the curriculum, schools can instill a solid ethical foundation in students, preparing them to become conscientious and compassionate members of society. This holistic approach to education not only fosters personal development but also contributes to the creation of a more harmonious and empathetic community. Therefore, incorporating value education in schools is essential for nurturing well-rounded individuals with strong moral principles.

The importance of reading storybooks

Reading storybooks is immensely important for individuals of all ages. These books not only offer an escape from the demands of everyday life but also provide valuable lessons, insights, and perspectives. They stimulate the imagination, improve concentration, and enhance language and cognitive skills. Moreover, storybooks expose readers to different cultures, experiences, and emotions, fostering empathy and understanding. Readers can explore diverse worlds, characters, and situations through stories, expanding their knowledge and awareness. Reading storybooks is a captivating and enriching endeavor that nourishes the mind and soul.

11. STORY WRITING

Story writing is an art. It is the oldest form of written composition. It is a **work of imagination** written in an easily comprehensible grammatical structure. A short story is meant to be read in a single sitting, so it should be as **direct and brief** as possible. A short story is **a fictional work of prose** that is ***much shorter in length than a novel***. In his essay 'The Philosophy of Composition,' Edgar Allan Poe said a short story should be read in one sitting.

A short story usually focuses on **one plot** and **one main character** (with a few additional minor characters), whereas a novel deals with many plots and many main characters, *such as heroes, heroines, villains, etc.*

Short stories ***contain underlying themes or motifs*** that lead readers to a broader conclusion from the material it has and encourage them to think beyond on a wider level about interconnected issues and topics of our natural world; thus, often, it tends to give a lesson.

Main Points related to Story Writing:

- Must have a Title: The story's title must be exciting and *evoke curiosity*.
- There must be an exciting theme in the story, which is the controlling idea of the story.
- A planned and logical series of events must be reflected in the story, and the events should not deviate from its central theme.
- The depiction of the characters must be engaging and convincing.
- The language of the story must be appropriate for the story and the setting.
- Many stories convey a moral lesson, too, at the end.

(1) Write a story in 120 words using the following hints. Give a title to the story:
[**Hints:** A fox fell into a well—failed to come out—a goat came—fox asked the goat to taste its water, very sweet—goat jumped in—fox climbed on goat's back and came out—got remained in the well— (moral lesson)]

A Fox and a Foolish Goat

Once, a fox wandered a village and fell into a shallow well. Although no water was present, it couldn't climb out. Shortly after, a thirsty goat approached the well. Seeing an opportunity, the fox convinced the goat to jump in for a taste of the supposedly sweet water. The unsuspecting goat lcapcd in, allowing thc fox to climb onto its back and escape from the well. The fox thanked the goat and departed, leaving the poor goat stranded in the well.

Keep Away Even from the Shadow of an Evil Person / Avoid the influence of deceitful individuals

(2) Use the following points and develop them into a story. Supply a suitable moral.
[**Hints:** Leelavati married a thief—a son, born—thief died—Leelavati married a businessman—he loved family, reared the child well—grew up, took charge of business—parents died—the last rites on the riverside—recognized mother's hands, but not father's—Betal asked Bikram, 'who is the real father?'—'the businessman'.
(write a moral lesson)]

'Who Is His Real Father'

Betal put forward a puzzle to Vikram. "A woman called Leelavati married a thief and had a son with him. Unfortunately, the thief passed away, and Leelavati then married a businessman. The businessman loved the family and raised the child well. When the child grew up, he took charge of the business. After the parents died, the last rites were performed by the riverside. During this time, the child recognized his mother's hands but couldn't identify his father's. Betal asked Bikram: "Who is his real father?" and Bikram answered, "The businessman."

Moral Lesson: The love and care given in upbringing hold more significance than biological parenthood.

Foster Parent is worthier than the Biological Parent in reality

(3) Study the outline and develop them into a story. You must give a title to your story:

A battle of wits between a mountain mouse and the mighty mountain—one said another, 'Poor little thing'—and itself boasted of its big size and ability to stop clouds—another politely agreed and said, 'But you can't stop me making big holes—mouse outwitted the mighty mountain.

The Mountain and the Mouse

Once upon a time, a mountain and a mouse fought a battle of wits. The mountain said, "What a poor little thing you are!" The mouse said, "I may not be as big as you are, but you're not as small as I am."

"Being big has its advantages," the mountain replied. "I can stop the clouds from sailing across the sky and make it rain upon me for the trees I carry on my shoulders."

"You're right," the mouse agreed. You can perform hefty tasks, but sorry to say, my friend, you can't stop me from making big holes in your very foundation, can you?" The tiny mouse outwitted the mighty mountain in the debate.

Big or Small, Each One Has Its unique Importance

(4) Read the points and develop them into a story. You must give a title to your story:

A lamb went to a stream—drinking water—a wolf made a plan to hunt—'You are making my water dirty'— 'But water flowing down to me!'—'You, the same rude fellow, abused me last year'—'I was not even born then'—'Then, it was your mom'—jumped and killed.

'The Wolf and the Lamb'

Once, a lamb went to a nearby stream to drink water. As he was drinking water, a wolf arrived there. He saw the lamb and thought, "The flesh of this little one must be sweet and soft. I must kill him to make my food." Thinking so, he began to find a suitable excuse to kill the animal. He went closer to the lamb and said, "You are making my drinking water dirty." The lamb said, "No, it can't be so because the water is flowing down to me from your end." "Don't argue with me," said the wolf. "Perhaps you are the same rude fellow who abused me last year." "But, I was not even born that time. How can it be me?" the innocent little lamb said meekly. The wolf said, "In that case, it must be your mother who had abused me last year. You must pay her offense." Saying so, the wolf jumped and killed the poor lamb.

Keep Away Even from the Shadow of an Evil Person

(5) Read the points and develop them into a story. You must give a title to your story:

Four cows lived in a jungle—fast friends—lived in peace—and fought against the enemy unitedly. A tiger had an eye—not dare to attack—one day, the cows fell out and went separately their own ways—the tiger got his opportunity—to kill them one by one.

Four Cows and a Tiger

Once upon a time, four cows lived in a jungle. They were fast friends, living and grazing together in peace. Whenever a wild animal attacked them, they unitedly fought against their enemy and drove it away.

A tiger had its eye on these cows because they were healthy and full of flesh, but it didn't dare to attack them as they lived united. However, one day, a quarrel developed among the cows over a piece of grass, and they separated. This separation gave the tiger the golden opportunity it had been waiting for. It killed the cows one by one and ate them up.

Unity Is Strength. United We Stand, Divided We Fall

(6) Read the points and develop them into a story. You must give a title to your story:

Two frogs fell into a churn of milk—swam round and round—tried to hop out—no solid support, so they couldn't—one out of his tiredness, gave up hope and drowned—the other kept itself floating—its movements turned the churn into butter—the frog climbed up on the pat of butter—hopped out.

Two Frogs in Churn of Milk

One day, two frogs fell into a churn of milk in a large jar. They swam round and round and tried to hop out, but no solid support was under their feet, preventing them from escaping.

After some time, one frog became exhausted and gave up, saying, "I can't swim any longer. I am giving up." It soon sank to the bottom of the churn and died. The other frog, however, persisted in its struggle. It continued swimming until the churn of milk turned into thick butter. The frog then climbed onto the pat of butter and hopped out of the churn to safety. The other frog, unfortunately, did not survive.

God Helps Those Who Help Themselves

(7) Read the points and develop them into a story. You must give a title to your story:

A farmer had a magic goose—laid a golden egg every day—the farmer became rich—built a large house, and lived with his wife and children—he planned to become very rich—and killed the goose to take all the eggs in it at a time—alas! --found nothing—the goose dead—he went mad.

The Farmer and the Magic Goose

Once upon a time, a farmer owned a magic goose. The goose would lay a golden egg daily, which the farmer sold at a good price. As time passed, the farmer became wealthy and built a large house where he lived with his wife and children. They enjoyed abundant food, exquisite clothing, and a spacious home. However, the farmer's greed grew, and he

hatched a wicked plan to kill the goose and obtain all its golden eggs to become the richest man in the entire state.
One morning, the farmer carried out his plan and killed the goose with a large knife, cutting open its belly. To his despair, there were no eggs or gold inside the goose. Overcome with regret and misery, he realized the folly of killing the magical goose.

Greed is the Root of All Evil that makes a man Devil!

(8) Read the points and develop them into a story. You must give a title to your story:

Summertime—bright and beautiful—plenty of food—grasshopper ate and spent time singing—an ant saved food for its future need—Winter came—scares of food—time came for grasshopper to starve—reached to the ant to beg for some food—the ant shut the door on her face, saying spend winter in dance, no food for lazy creatures.

The Grasshopper and the Ant

In the summer, everything is bright and beautiful. Food is plentiful. A grasshopper eats to its heart's content and sings merrily, hopping here and there. One day, she saw her friend collecting and carrying food. She asked him where he was carrying the piece of corn and seed. The ant said it was for his future plans. The grasshopper began to laugh at him, calling him a fool and advising him to live in the present.

Summer went by, and gradually, winter arrived at the door. Food was getting scarce for everybody. The grasshopper found it challenging to get food for herself, and at last, the time came for her almost to starve. So, one day, the grasshopper knocked at the door of her friend, the ant. She requested that he give her something to eat. The ant said, "You spent the summer singing merrily, doing almost nothing. Now you spend the winter dancing. I won't give anything to a lazy creature like you," he shut his door in her face.

Save Today's Surpluses for Tomorrow's Needs

(9) Read the points and develop them into a story. You must give a title to your story:

An eagle had his nest high up on a mountain wall—near the foothill, a crow's nest on a branch of a tree— one day, the eagle swooped down and picked up a lamb—the crow thought to act the same—on another, he too flew high up—swooped down—broke his head and beak—made its tragic end.

The Dangerous Feat by a Crow

An eagle had built its nest high up on a mountain wall. At the foot of the mountain, a crow lived in a tree. One day, the eagle swooped down from its nest and picked up a lamb from the earth. Then, it flew high up and returned to its nest. The crow saw the eagle perform this incredible feat and thought, "If the eagle can do it, why can't I?" So, one day, the crow flew as high as it could and then swooped down with great force. However, the crow dashed against the ground instead of picking up a lamb, cracking its head and beak. And that was the end of the crow.

Measure your weight before an act

(10) Read the points and develop them into a story. You must give a title to your story:

Two boys walking along a road—saw a nut on the ground—one picked it up and said, 'It is mine.' Another said, 'It's mine, for I saw it first—third one entered the scene—wanted to settle the quarrel—cracked nut—separated its hard shell into two parts—divided the shell equally—devoured the fruit seed, saying—the charge of the settlement.

Two Stupid Boys and a Nut

One day, two boys were walking along a road when they saw a nut on the ground. Both of them ran quickly to pick it up. One boy grabbed it and claimed, "It is mine." The other boy argued, "It is my nut because I saw it first." A third boy passing by noticed the quarrel and intervened, offering to settle the dispute. Both agreed, and the boy holding the nut gave it to him. The third boy cracked the nut, divided its hard shell into two equal parts, and gave each boy a part. He then ate the fruit seed, declaring, "This is the cost of the settlement."

When Two Persons Quarrel, A Third Person Gains

(11) Read the points and develop them into a story. You must give a title to your story:

two cats – hungry – a loaf of bread – greedy—each one wanted to divide, & silently wished for a more significant portion– quarrels began – a clever monkey – offered his help – bit by bit – finally, no piece of bread – demanded his fee – two foolish cats went away silently – remained hungry that day.

Equal Share

Once upon a time, two cats lived in a village. One day, they were starving and searched for food but could not find anything. They soon spotted a loaf of bread beside a shop. Each of them was greedy and wanted a bigger portion of the bread. They fought over who would divide the bread, and their quarrel drew the attention of a passing monkey. The clever monkey offered to help settle the dispute. He broke the bread into two uneven sizes and then ate a portion from the larger share to make it equal to the other. However, the cats were unhappy, and the dispute continued. In a few minutes, both portions of bread were gone. The monkey then demanded his fees. The two cats realized their folly and went away silently unfed.

When Two Quarrel, a Third One Looks for Chance

(12) Read the points and develop them into a story. You must give a title to your story:

A bear, a wolf, a fox, and a lion went hunting —killed a buffalo—the fox divided it into four parts—waiting eagerly for their shares—the lion roared—claimed one part, being a partner—2nd part for leadership—3rd part for its cubs—for the next and last he welcomed everyone for combat.

The Lion's Share

Once, a bear, a wolf, and a fox went hunting under the leadership of a lion. Very soon, they caught and killed a buffalo. The fox divided the buffalo into four parts. The animals were eagerly waiting to eat their shares. The lion roared, "Keep away from the prey and listen to me. I claim one part of the prey because I was your partner in hunting. I claim a second part of it because I was your leader. I claim a third part because I want it for my cubs. If anyone wants a share of the fourth part, come and fight me for it." The bear, the wolf, and the fox let the lion have all four parts of the prey and walked away quietly without saying a word from the place. After all, who wants to be the lion's next prey on that day?

Might Is Right

(13) Read the points and develop them into a story. You must give a title to your story:

A ***country mouse*** and a ***town mouse*** made friends—the country mouse invited his friend—and served the best berries, nuts and roots—town mouse did not like the food, saying it ***poor and tasteless***—he invited—the other accepted —served figs, dates, honey, biscuits—really rich and delicious—but couldn't eat—a cat arrived—they took shelter in a narrow hole—the country mouse went back—at least, he can eat peacefully in her home in the village.

The Country Mouse and the Town Mouse

Once upon a time, there was a friendship between a country mouse and a town mouse. The country mouse lived in a vast green field, while the town mouse lived in a house. One day, the country mouse invited the town mouse for dinner and served the best berries, nuts, and roots. However, the town mouse did not like the simple country food and invited the country mouse to visit his house in town. There, the town mouse served figs, dates, honey, biscuits, bread, and jam, which the country mouse found rich and delicious. Just as they were about to eat, a cat arrived, causing both mice to flee to a narrow hole. Feeling uncomfortable, the country mouse remarked on the town mouse's life, expressing a wish for the town mouse to live in the village where he could eat peacefully without fear of the cat. The town mouse could not reply.

Riches Do Not Always Bring Happiness.

(14) Read the points and develop them into a story. You must give a title to your story:

Once, a cat and a fox discussing hounds (hunting dogs) —hounds run very fast—"They can't catch me ever, for I know many tricks," said the fox— 'I know only one trick,' said the cat—the fox laughed at him—soon hounds were after the fox—played many tricks—the cat ran up a nearby tree—the fox ran along thorny hedge—hid amidst thick bushes and in burrows—finally, it was caught and killed—the cat murmured, mine one is the best.

Whose trick is the Best, a Cat & a Fox

Once upon a time, a cat and a fox discussed their tricks to escape from hounds. "They are swift runners," said the fox, "but they can never catch me; I know many tricks to get rid of them." "What tricks do you have? Tell me something," asked the cat. "I have a lot of tricks," boasted the fox. "I can run along a thorny hedge, hide amidst thick bushes, and even shelter in burrows. These are just a few of the many tricks I know," said the fox. "I only know one good trick," the cat said. "How sad! Only one trick? What is it?" asked the fox. Before the cat could reply, some hounds arrived. They were after the fox. The fox tried to show all his tricks. He ran along a thorny hedge, hid amidst thick bushes, and took shelter in a burrow. Meanwhile, the cat smoothly climbed a tall tree and watched everything from the top. None of the fox's tricks worked, and he was eventually caught and killed by the hounds. Witnessing the fox's demise, the cat murmured, "Mine is the best of all those fruitless tricks of the poor fox!"

Mastery in one Art Is Better Than being a Jack of All Trades

(15) Read the points and develop them into a story. You must give a title to your story:

A farmer, five sons—strong and hardworking—but they quarreled—farmer, unhappy—wanted his sons to be united—farmer tricked a plan—called everyone and asked them to bring sticks—chose fifteen—asked to tie them to make a bundle—asked them to break the bundle—none could—they got the lesson—farmer died happily after years.

A Farmer and His Five Sons

A farmer had five solid and hardworking sons, but they constantly quarreled among themselves, which made the farmer very unhappy. He wanted his sons to stop quarreling and live happily and peacefully, so he made a plan. One day, he called them all and asked them to bring some sticks for him. He chose fifteen sticks and asked them to tie them up to make a bundle. His sons obeyed, but they had a lot of questions in their minds. The farmer asked each son to try to break the bundle of sticks, but they couldn't. Then he asked them to untie the bundle and break a stick, which they easily could without any particular force. The farmer then explained the lesson to his sons, and they promised not to fight anymore. After this, they no longer quarreled, developed a good understanding, and learned to be patient and sacrifice their little needs. This made the farmer very happy, and he died one day happily.

United We Stand, Divided We Fall

(16) Read the points and develop them into a story. You must give a title to your story:

Once the wind and the sun argued—who is stronger—a traveler walking, wrapped in a cloak—who can detach his clock from him be declared to be the winner, i.e., stronger—both agreed to the condition —the wind blew harder—the man held the clock tighter—wind's turn over—the sun smiled warmly— the man let the clock loose and open—sun grew warmer—he took the clock off —the sun was declared to be stronger.

'Who is stronger, the Wind and the Sun?'

Once, the wind and the sun got into an argument. "I am stronger than you," said the Wind. "No, you are not," said the Sun. While arguing, a traveler passed by, wrapped in a cloak because it was winter. The wind suggested, 'Whoever of us can get the traveler's cloak off should be declared the stronger.' The sun agreed. The wind went first, blowing harder and harder, but the traveler only held his cloak tighter. When the wind's turn was over, the Sun started shining warmly, and the traveler started feeling the warmth. The Sun shone even brighter, and the traveler took off his cloak and hung it on his shoulder. The Sun was declared the stronger of the two.

Brute Force Can't Achieve What a Gentle Smile Can.

(17) Read the points and develop them into a story. You must give a title and moral to your story:

A grocer's shop—lived many mice—plenty of food: grains, dry fruits, bread, and biscuits, etc.—the grocer suffered heavy loss—brought a cat—hunted mice every day—other mice worried—held a meeting to get rid of the cat—a smart young mouse suggested tying a bell round the neck—all began to rejoice—an old mouse stood up and said, who will bell the cat? –silence prevailed—none wanted to sacrifice his or her life.

To Bell the Cat

A grocer owned a shop where many mice lived. The shop had plenty of food, such as grains, dry fruits, bread, and biscuits. However, the grocer suffered heavy losses due to the mice. To solve this problem, the grocer brought a cat to hunt the mice daily. The other mice became worried and held a meeting to figure out how to get rid of the cat. A bright young mouse suggested they tie a bell around the cat's neck. Everyone began to rejoice at this idea, but an old mouse stood up and asked, "Who will bell the cat?" This made the other mice silent, realizing that none wanted to sacrifice their life to bell the cat.

Moral: It's easy to suggest a solution, but it's much harder to find someone willing to implement it.

or

Impractical Solutions are not worthy of Rejoice

(18) Read the points and develop them into a story. You must give a title and moral to your story:

A fox saw a cock sitting on a tree—thought it a good meal—but could not climb—wanted the cock to come down—made a plan, and said, "Beasts & birds are now friends from Heaven's law"—need not be afraid of—cock informed of coming 'hounds'—the word made the fox flee at once.

'Beasts & Birds are now Friends,' a Fox to a Cock

Sample 1

Once, a fox saw a cock sitting high up on a tree. "What a good meal he could be for me!" thought the fox. But he could not climb up a tree. He wanted the cock to come down on the ground. So, the fox sat under the tree and said, "Hello, cock. I have some good news for you. There is an order from Heaven. Now, all the birds and beasts shall live as friends. They shall not eat each other. Fox will not eat cocks and hens. So, you need not be afraid of me now. Please come down. We shall sit and talk together." The cock said, "That is good news indeed. I can see some of your friends coming to meet you." "My friends? Who are they?" asked the fox in surprise. The cock said, "Hounds." The word 'hounds' filled the fox with fear. He sprang up on his four legs and was ready to run away. The cock said, "Why should you be afraid of them? We all are friends now." "I know that," said the fox. "But, perhaps, hounds do not know this." Soon, the fox fled into the deep forest.

Sample 2

A fox spotted a rooster perched on a tree and decided it would make a delicious meal. However, the fox couldn't climb the tree, so it tried to persuade the rooster to come down. The fox devised a plan and told the rooster, "Animals and birds are now friends according to the laws of nature, so there's no need to be afraid." The rooster then warned the fox about the approaching hounds, causing the fox to flee immediately.

(80 words)

Do Not Put Blind Faith in The Words of Cunning People

(19) Read the points and develop them into a story. Write also the title and a moral to the story. [A hungry fox – saw a crow with a piece of meat in its beak—made a plan – praised the crow of its sweet voice – the crow felt very happy –began to sing – the piece of meat fell– Fox picked up – ran away.]

The Cunning Fox and the Crow

Once, on a sunny day in the forest, a hungry fox spotted a crow perched on a branch, holding a delicious piece of meat in its beak. The mischievous fox, known for its cunning ways, devised a plan to trick the unsuspecting crow. In a smooth and flattering tone, the fox lavished praise upon the crow, specifically admiring its melodious voice. Flattered by the unexpected compliment, the crow, eager to demonstrate its vocal talent, opened its beak and released a beautiful song. However, amid its joyful singing, the prized meat slipped from its beak and fell to the ground below. Seizing the opportunity, the sly fox snatched up the tasty morsel and swiftly fled before the crow realized what had happened.

Do not let flattery cloud your judgment.

(20) Read the points and develop them into a story. You must give a title to your story:

A crow sitting on a tree—a piece of meat in its beak—fox passing under the tree—wants the meat—asks the crow to sing—crow keeps meat under its feet and sings—befooled, fox leaves the place.

'How Sweet is your Voice!' A Fox to a Crow

Once, a crow stole a piece of meat from a butcher's shop. A clever fox passed by while sitting on a tree branch with the meat in its beak. The fox tricked the crow by praising its voice and asking it to sing a song. The crow saw through the trick, carefully placed the meat on the branch, held it with its feet, and began to sing 'caw, caw.' The fox, tired of the crow's cawing, left the place stealthily, and the crow then ate its meat happily.

Praise without Base may be Deceiving

(21) Read the points and develop them into a story. You must give a title to your story:

A small boy Johny—always eager to show his wit—one morning, he went to a barber—asked in a grim voice for a shave—barber wrapped a cloth around his neck—gave soap all over his face—got busy in other work waiting for him there—after a long time, Johny made in shout, 'why keeping me wait'—'waiting for your beard to come out, little master,' he said.

Little Johny at the Barber

A small boy named Johnny was always eager to show his wit. One morning, he decided to play a trick on the barber in his neighborhood. He went to the barber's shop and sat in a chair before a mirror. The barber asked, "Yes, Johnny?" Johnny said sternly, "Will you please shave my beard?" The barber saw through the game, but he remained silent. Instead, he politely said, "I will surely do so, young master."

The barber then put a piece of cloth around Johnny's shoulders and applied soap to his face. Then he got busy with some other work. Johnny waited long, finding it difficult to stay with soap all over his face. After an hour, he shouted at the barber, "Why are you keeping me waiting?" The barber smiled and replied coldly, "I'm waiting for your beard to come out, young master." Johnny understood his folly. After cleaning his face, Johnny apologized to the barber and returned home stealthily.

When You Play a Joke on Someone, Others may play on You, too.

(22) Read the points and develop them into a story. You must give a title to your story:

A crooked tree in a forest—had a trunk, many branches and odd-snapped—when others had straight and fine—' how unlucky I am,' uttered the tree—a woodcutter came — looked at the crooked tree & said, 'it is entirely useless' and went away—selected others & cut them down—the crooked tree, saved —no more he felt sad—its ugliness saved it from the axe.

The Crooked Tree

A crooked tree was among many tall and straight trees in a forest. Its trunk and branches were bent oddly, unlike the straight, sharp trees around it. The crooked tree looked at them and said, "How fine and straight they are!" Then it added in a sad voice, "How unlucky I am! Why am I the only one that is crooked and ugly among them?" One day, a woodcutter came to the forest. He looked at the crooked tree and said, "This tree is useless for me." He selected all the tall and straight trees and cut them down. The crooked tree no longer felt sad about its appearance, for it realized that its crookedness saved it from the woodcutter's axe.

"Be happy with who you are and what you have."

(23) Read the points and develop them into a story. You must give a title and a moral to your story:

Two women quarreled over a tiny baby—each claimed to be its mother—and the case was brought before Akbar. The emperor found it challenging. Both showered love and affection—thought a little—gave orders to cut the baby into two parts—both ghastly amazed—when his man approached the baby, a woman screamed and gave up her claim—the other remained calm—Akbar recognized the real mother—punished the other.

The Real Mother

Once, two women quarreled over a tiny baby. Each claimed that she was the mother of the child. They were brought before Akbar, the emperor of the Mughal Empire. Akbar listened to both of the women. He found it difficult when both women showed their love and affection equally to the little child. However, Akbar pondered a few more seconds, and he ordered his men, "Cut the baby into two equal parts and give each part to the woman." Both the women were ghastly amazed at the strange order. When Akbar's man approached the little child, a woman suddenly screamed and said, "Mercy, Your Lordship. Let that woman have the child. Let the poor thing live. I give up my claim to it." While the other woman remained quiet. Akbar instantly recognized its natural mother. He ordered his man to give the baby to the woman who was ready to give up her claim. And he sent the other woman to jail.

Truth Always Triumphs

(24) Read the points and develop them into a story. You must give a title to your story:

An idiot—even a village child could cheat him—once he, going to the weekly market to sell his horse and a goat—hung a bell from a collar around the goat's neck—tied one end of the rope with it—and another end to the horse's tail— mounting the horse, rode for the market—three rogues followed—one untied the bell from goat's neck—tied it too to the horse's tail—kept ringing—another rogue stopped him—why have you tied the bell with horse's tail—the third one arrived, suggested for ride and catch the man with goat—the idiot began wait—none returned— he returned home empty hand.

An Idiot and Three Rogues

Once upon a time, in a village, there lived an easily deceived man. No matter how hard he tried to be clever, someone always made a fool of him. One day, the man was going to the weekly market to sell his horse and goat. He tied one end of a rope to the horse's tail and the other to the goat's collar, then hung a bell on the goat's collar. As he rode to the marketplace, three rogues followed him, planning to steal his horse and goat. One of the rogues tied the bell to the horse's tail and ran away with the goat. The bell made the man believe the goat was still following him. Later, another rogue stopped the man and asked why a bell was tied to the horse's tail. The man, realizing his goat was missing, was shocked. Then, the third rogue offered to chase the thief on the man's horse. The man believed him, gave him the horse, and the rogue rode away. Eventually, the second rogue escaped, and none of them returned. The man realized he had been tricked and returned home empty-handed. Meanwhile, the rogues sang a song with the lyrics, "Jingle bell, jingle bell, jingle all the way; keep on singing day and night; life is but a play."

Moral: A Fool and His Fortune Don't Stay Together for A Long Time.

(25) Read the points and develop them into a story. You must give a title to your story:

A tall tree—a little black bird—sang sweetly—fell grains of gold on the ground—a fowler—caught the bird—became rich getting grains of gold every day—wanted name and fame—made a cage of gold—gifted the bird with the golden cage to the king—king became richer—king gave it to his beloved queen—the queen set the bird free & the cage to a goldsmith to make beautiful ornaments— the bird now sings 'the song of four fools' who wasted their fortune.

The Song of Four Fools

A little black bird lived in a tall tree in a jungle. Every morning, it sang sweetly, and a few grains of gold fell from its beak as it sang. One morning, a fowler (bird hunter) saw the gold grains dropping from its beak and thought of the fortune he could have if he caught the bird. He spread a net on the ground and sprinkled some rice grains to trap the bird. The black bird flew into the net, and the fowler caught it and took it home.

Every day, the fowler received a few grains of gold from the bird and became rich. Wanting fame and honor, he made a beautiful gold cage and presented the bird and the cage to the King, claiming that the bird would sing sweet songs and give grains of gold every day. The King was pleased and gave the fowler a seat of honor in his court. The king also became very wealthy due to the gold grains from the bird.

After some time, the King gave the cage and the bird to his beloved queen, who set the bird free and gave the cage to the royal goldsmith, asking for the most beautiful ornament to be made from it. The bird flew back into the jungle and sang "The Song of Four Fools" every morning: "I flew into the Fowler's net. I was the **first fool**. The Fowler gave me away to the king. The fowler was the **second fool**. The King gave me away to the queen. The king was the **third fool**. The queen set me free. The queen was the **fourth fool** who gave me freedom at the cost of her fortune."

"When fortune favors, why let it go? Fortune changes hands constantly."

(26) Read the points and develop them into a story. You must give a title to your story:

Japanese Emperor—had a set of twenty flowerpots—finest and rare collection—emperor's favorite—one day, an officer broke one by accident—death sentence passed—before execution, an old man came—told, knew the art of repairing—taken to flowerpots—the man broke all with his stick at once—emperor's wrath knew no bound—enquired why he did—calmly the old man replied—one pot taking one's life, I broke all, now it would take only mine—emperor thought—realized his folly—forgave both—emperor would respect the man's bravery and wisdom.

The Emperor, Wise Old Man & Twenty Flower Pots

A Japanese emperor owned twenty flowerpots, the world's finest collection of their kind and his favorite. One day, a palace officer accidentally broke one of the flowerpots, angering the emperor. He immediately sentenced the officer to death. Before the execution, an old man appeared in the emperor's court and claimed he could repair the broken flowerpot to look as good as new. The emperor, happy at the possibility, showed the old man his collection of flowerpots and the broken one and promised to pay him whatever he asked for if he could repair it.

However, to the surprise of everyone present, the old man raised his stick and broke all the nineteen remaining flowerpots before anyone could stop him. Enraged, the emperor demanded an explanation for this act and threatened the old man with immediate execution. The old man calmly responded, "Your Majesty, I have done my duty. Each of these flowerpots would have taken one human life. Now, you can take only one life, and that is mine."

The emperor, struck by the old man's wisdom and boldness, realized his mistake in valuing mere earthen pots. He forgave both the officer and the old man, sparing them from the sentence of death, and ordered them to clear the dust before leaving the spot.

Forgiveness is greater than giving Punishment / Human life is more worthy than a thing of frail.

(27) Read the points and develop them into a story. You must give a title to your story:

A village moneylender lost his purse—announced a reward of hundred rupees—a poor farmer found it—needy but honest—returned the purse to moneylender—moneylender counted and called him a 'smart fellow'—one hundred is missing—i.e., he has taken his reward beforehand—poor man felt insulted—the farmer brought the case to sarpanch (the village head)—sarpanch realized the moneylender to be dishonest—if you are sure, it had eleven hundred, the purse is not yours—give the purse to the farmer.

The Moneylender and His Purse

Once, a village moneylender lost his purse. He announced a reward of a hundred rupees to the person who would find and return it to him. A poor farmer found it, and to his surprise, it contained one thousand rupees. Despite being in need, the farmer did the right thing and returned the purse to the moneylender.

Upon receiving the purse, the moneylender counted the money inside and found one thousand rupees. He then said to the farmer, "You are a smart fellow. You have taken your reward beforehand." The farmer was puzzled and asked for an explanation. The moneylender claimed that the purse originally contained eleven hundred rupees, implying that the farmer had taken the reward money.

Feeling insulted and being confident in his honesty, the farmer suggested to go to the Sarpanch (the head of the village committee) to settle the matter. After hearing both sides, the Sarpanch was convinced that the moneylender was lying. He then instructed the moneylender to return the purse to the farmer.

Moral: A Wrongdoer to Pay a Heavy Price / Honesty is the best policy

(28) Read the points and develop them into a story. You must give a title to your story:

A salt vendor had a donkey—loaded the donkey with bags of salt every day—had customers in surrounding villages—had to cross rivers and streams—one day, the donkey accidentally fell into a small river—load became lighter—trip canceled—from next day, the donkey did tricks—the master realized— thought for a lesson—loaded with bales of cotton—crossing river—donkey took a dip—load became many times heavier—struggled too much—the donkey didn't repeat the action.

The Salt Vendor and His Donkey

A salt vendor had a donkey. Every morning, he loaded the donkey with bags of salt, and together, they went to visit customers in surrounding villages. On the way, they had to cross several streams and small rivers. One morning, the donkey accidentally tumbled into a river, causing much of the salt in the bags to dissolve in the water, making the burden on the donkey's back much lighter. The vendor and the donkey returned home, and the donkey had a rest day.

The next day, as they set out on their usual trip, the donkey intentionally took a dip in the first stream, making the burden light again and causing the trip to be canceled again. The vendor got angry but didn't say anything, thinking, "I must teach him a lesson." The following day, he decided to load the donkey with bales of cotton. When the donkey repeated the mischief while crossing a river, the cotton absorbed water, making the load much heavier. The donkey had to struggle very hard to come out of the water. From that day onwards, the donkey gave up the trick of dipping in a stream.

Mischiefs can't make one Rich and Prosperous

(29) Read the points and develop them into a story. You must give a title to your story:

Defeated King Bruce—shelter in a cave —sad and dejected—noticed a spider—tried to make a cobweb—fell again and again—finally, succeeded—king thought for another fight—met his followers—built a strong and large army—won battle.

The King Robert Bruce and the Spider

Once, the king of Scotland, Robert the Bruce, was defeated in a battle in the early 14th century. He took shelter in a cave in the jungle, feeling sad and dejected as his enemies were more powerful. His courage and confidence had left him. Suddenly, he noticed a tiny spider trying to make a cobweb from the ceiling on the cave walls. It fell again and again, but it kept on its attempts. On its twelfth try, it made the cobweb from the ceiling to the wall. This incident inspired the King, and he decided to build an army against his enemies. He emerged from his shelter, gathered his fellowmen, and built a large, strong army. Then, he declared war and attacked his enemies repeatedly until he won the battle. The king was happy to regain his lost kingdom. He uttered a few words to thank the little creature and for its lesson for the king.

Moral: Success Comes to Those Who Fight Hard Against Failures.

(30) Read the points and develop them into a story. You must give a title to your story:

'How many crows in the city?'–emperor Akbar to courtiers—to test their wits—None could answer—Birbal, the wittiest, entered—same question to him—Birbal replied instant—fifty thousand three hundred and seventy-eight—let all in great amazement!—how? — Birbal explained if some more, it's due to friends and relatives of crows visited; if less, some have visited their friends and relatives elsewhere—the reply pleased the emperor—"Birbal, you are matchless indeed!"

How Many Crows in The City: Akbar & Birbal

Once, Emperor Akbar thought of a riddle for his courtiers to test their wits for fun. He said, "My court is full of wise men, and I can't find an answer." All the courtiers asked, "What, your majesty?" Akbar said, "It haunts me from this dawn today, 'How many crows are in my city?' Some of them caw beside my palace all through the day." Listening to the emperor's question, the courtiers looked at each other, trying to figure out the answer. None of them could answer. During this challenging hour, the Emperor's wise man, Birbal, arrived at the court. The same question was asked of him, and he promptly replied, "Your majesty, there are only fifty thousand three hundred and seventy-eight crows in this city." The Emperor was astonished and asked, "How can you say that? And how can you be sure?"

Birbal replied, "Please have them counted, my lord. If there are more than fifty thousand three hundred and seventy-eight crows, it is simply due to some crows that might have come from elsewhere to visit their friends and relatives in this city. If there are fewer, it must be some crows from this city that have visited their friends and relatives elsewhere, near or far." The emperor was pleased with Birbal's response and exclaimed, "You are matchless, Birbal, among all!"

Presence of Wits Is Sometimes Greater Than Proper Knowledge and Information

(31) Read the points and develop them into a story. You must give a title to your story:

Hot summer day—a traveler hired a donkey—wanted to go next town—donkey was lazy—its master flogged the animal to keep it moving—stopped on the way to rest—traveler sat in the shade of donkey—master also very tired—wanted to sit in the shade—no shade nearby—began a quarrel over the right of shadow—donkey ran away—they lost both donkey and its shadow.

The Donkey and his Shadow

It was a hot summer day. A traveler hired a donkey to carry him across the dusty road to the next town. The donkey was lazy and stopped now and then, so his master walked behind and flogged the animal to keep him moving. At noon, they stopped to rest. The traveler sat in the donkey's shadow to escape the heat. When the donkey's master asked to share the shade, the traveler refused, claiming that since he rented the donkey, he had the right to use its shadow. This led to a heated argument, during which the donkey ran away, taking its shadow with it. Both men had to run after the donkey in the sun's scorching heat.

Moral: Those Who Fight Over a Shadow Lose the Substance true to Life and all

Or

(Those who fight over substance or worldliness lose both relation & spiritualism)

(32) Read the points and develop them into a story. You must give a title to your story:

A long time ago—in a fight between birds and beasts—bats didn't join either side—looking for a chance—they had both reasons—can fly like birds—but neither having wings nor laying eggs—when beasts seemed to get win—bats joined them—but soon birds got the better of the beasts—bats changed parties—finally, birds and beasts made peace and became friends—both boycotted selfish bats—bats went off—hid in dark holes—live there since—come out only in twilight—when birds and beasts in their respective nests and dens at night.

Bats, the Fair-weather Friends

Once upon a time, there was a conflict between the birds and the beasts. The bats chose not to align with either side. They reasoned, "We can't join the birds because we don't lay eggs like them, and we can't join the beasts because we have wings like the birds." They believed their position was unique and decided to wait and watch to join the winners later. As the fighting continued, the beasts appeared to emerge victorious, so the bats joined them. However, as the tide turned in favor of the birds, the bats regretted their decision and switched sides. Ultimately, the birds and the beasts reconciled and became friends, leaving the bats ostracized. The self-centered bats retreated to dark caves and hidden holes, only venturing out at twilight when the birds and beasts had retired for the night.

Moral: Nobody Likes a Fair-Weather Friend

(33) Read the points and develop them into a story. You must give a title to your story:

One evening, a poor farm worker—on his way home—attracted by pleasant smell—coming from a sweetmeat shop—his mouth watered; he went there—stood sometime—not afford to buy—while he turned to go—shop keeper demanded payment for smell—stood a wise man nearby—whispered some to his ear—face lit up—went up to shop keeper—jingled some coins—'come on, pay the money'—'but, I have already paid you,' —how? — "Didn't you hear the jingle of the money? If smell is as good as eating, hearing is as good as receiving—and he walked away.

The Jingle of the Money

One evening, a poor farm worker was on his way home when he stopped beside the road. A pleasant smell was coming from a sweetmeat shop nearby, making his mouth water. Despite his desire to buy, he couldn't afford it and started to walk away. However, the shopkeeper demanded payment, claiming that enjoying the smell was as good as eating the sweet meat. Feeling trapped, the poor man was fortunate to have a wise man nearby. After receiving a whispered suggestion from the wise man, the poor man cleverly jingled a few coins in his pocket and claimed he had already paid for the sweetmeat, stating that if smelling is as good as eating, hearing is as good as receiving. With a smile, he walked away, proud of his clever solution and thankful for the wise man's help.

Moral: Tit for Tat

(34) Read the points and develop them into a story. You must give a title to your story:

An old woman—had a cock & two servants—woman woke up with crowing of cock every day and let her servants wake up too—servants wished for undisturbed sleep—killed the cock—no cock, no crowing—an old woman now would not know exact time—when she woke up, she made her servants awake too—even earlier than before.

An Old woman and her Servants

An old woman had two servants. Every day the woman would wake up as soon as her cock started crowing. Then, she would wake her servants and ask them to begin the day's work. The servants did not like to get up early in the morning. They wished undisturbed sleep in the morning. They began thinking about how to get rid of the cock and rising early in the morning. One day one servant said to the other, *"Let us kill the cock. If there is no cock, there will be no crowing. If there is no crowing, the mistress won't wake up early. If she does not wake up early, no one will disturb our quiet sleep."* As they thought, they killed the cock. Now, there was no cock; the old woman would not know the exact time. She would wake up even earlier than before. Once she woke up, she would not let her servants remain in bed. The cock was gone. But the servants had a more challenging time than before.

Moral: A Wrong Remedy Is Worse Than the Disease

(35) Read the points and develop them into a story. You must give a title to your story:

Some little frogs, playing at the edge of a pool—a bull came to drink water— bellowed loudly— the frogs frightened, hopped away—grandma asked—what was the matter—said of very big animal and its terrible sound— grandma parted his legs wide and puffed out her checks and all side—was that as big—no, much, much bigger than this—puffed more and more—lungs burst and fell dead.

The Bull and the Frogs

Once upon a time, some little frogs played at the edge of a pool. A bull came to drink water from the pool, and after finishing, he let out a loud bellow that frightened the frogs. They quickly hopped back to their grandma and explained what had happened. The grandma asked them how big the animal was, and the little frogs described it as very big. The grandma, trying to show them an animal even bigger, puffed out her cheeks and asked if the animal was as big as that. However, the frogs insisted that the animal was much, much bigger. The grandma kept puffing, and eventually, her efforts caused her lungs to burst, and she fell down dead.

Moral: Vanity Is Foolishness.

(36) Read the points and develop them into a story. You must give a title to your story:

A rich merchant came to Birbal—said, 'Someone of seven servants—stolen my bag of precious pearls. Please find out—Birbal went to—gave each one a magic stick, telling it would grow by one inch by next day who was a thief—next day, among the collected sticks, one was found one inch short—thief was found and sent to jail.

Birbal & his Magic Sticks

Once, a wealthy merchant approached Birbal, a renowned counselor of Emperor Akbar known for his wisdom. The merchant sought Birbal's help in finding the servant who had stolen his precious bag of pearls from among his seven servants. Birbal visited the merchant's house and gathered all the servants in a room. He then handed each of them a stick and claimed that these were magic sticks of equal length at that moment. He instructed the servants to keep and return the sticks the next day. Birbal declared that if a thief existed among them, his stick would grow an inch longer by the following day. Fearful of being caught, the guilty servant cut a piece of one inch from his stick to evade suspicion. The next day, Birbal collected the sticks from the servants and discovered that one was short by an inch. Birbal pointed at the servant with the shorter stick and accused him of being the thief. Faced with this accusation, the servant confessed his crime and returned the stolen bag of pearls. As a result, he was sent to jail.

Moral: A furtive mind is afraid of even a nail

(37) Read the points and develop them into a story. You must give a title to your story:

Tortoise and hare – good friends – tortoise, known for his slow speed – hare has fast speed – makes fun of tortoise – challenges him – referee selected – race starts – hare thought to take rest, and the race to begin afresh – takes a nap – tortoise wins.

The Race between Tortoise and Hare

Once, there lived a tortoise and a hare in a forest. They were good friends. The tortoise was known for his slow speed, while the hare was proud of his fast speed and often made fun of his friend's slow pace. One day, the tortoise challenged the hare to a race, and the hare agreed instantly. A horse was selected as the referee, and the race started. The hare ran very fast and soon reached far ahead of the tortoise. Tired and confident of winning, the hare decided to nap under a large tree beside a lake. Meanwhile, the tortoise continued and eventually passed the sleeping hare, reaching almost the finishing point. It was too late when the hare woke up and realized the tortoise was near the finish line. The slow but steady tortoise touched the finishing point and was declared the winner by the horse.

Moral: 'Slow but Steady wins the race.

(38) Read the points and develop them into a story. You must give a title to your story:

Bunya, a cowboy—drove cattle of villagers of Baptail—a wood nearby—believed to be visited often by a tiger—One day, the cowboy played mischief—cried, saying 'tiger, tiger, tiger'—villagers rushed to the spot—only to find him laughing at them—this repeated more than once—really a tiger approached another day—he cried for 'help, help, help'—None came to his aid—met his tragic end.

A Cow Boy and a Tiger

Once, a poor cowboy named Bunya lived in a village called Baptail, located near a wood. Bunya had lost his father in childhood, so he worked for others by herding cows and goats for the villagers in exchange for food and pay. Bunya loved to graze the cattle near the woods, where there was plenty of grass. However, there were rumors of a tiger living in the woods, although it hadn't been seen recently, leading some to believe there was no tiger there.

One day, Bunya decided to play a trick on the villagers. He shouted "tiger, tiger, tiger" at the top of his voice, pretending there was a tiger nearby to fool them. Many rushed to the woods with sticks, scythes, and other tools to help him, only to find Bunya laughing at how easily he had fooled them. Although some villagers got irritated, they said nothing because Bunya was grazing their cattle.

However, Bunya repeated the trick, which annoyed many villagers, who wanted to beat him, but others stopped them. Despite this, they vowed never to be made fun of by Bunya again.

A few days later, Bunya was again near the wood with his cattle. The animals were grazing, and Bunya was unaware of an approaching tiger. When he noticed the tiger, he screamed for help, but nobody came. Everyone thought he was trying to fool them again. Tragically, Bunya became the tiger's first prey that day while his cattle ran away.

"Never tell a lie".

(39) Write a story in about 100 words using the following points. Give a suitable title to your story:

[**Hints:** Two friends — passing through a forest — a bear appeared —one climbed up a tree — the other, helpless—lay down as a dead man— the bear came—sniffed & thought the boy dead— went away —the friend on the tree climbed down — inquired — what did the bear tell him — replied — "Don't trust a false friend."]

Two Friends & a Bear

Two friends were walking through a forest when a large black bear appeared about two hundred meters away. Both friends were very scared. One of them quickly climbed up a nearby tree, but the other friend didn't know how to climb and instead lay down like a dead man on the grass. The bear approached him, sniffed, and, thinking the boy was dead, went away. When the friend who had climbed the tree came down, he asked what the bear had whispered in his ear. The friend replied, "The bear warned me, 'Don't trust a false friend.'"

A Friend in Need is a Friend Indeed

(40) Write a story in about 100 words using the following points. Give a suitable title to the story:

[**Hints:** A king, proud of his power—says he can control everything on earth—takes his courtiers to the sea shore—orders the waves to move back—the waves lash at the feet of the king—the king moves back in fear.]

False Pride

Once upon a time, there lived a king in a kingdom. The king was known for his pride and foolishness. One day, he declared, "I can control everything on the earth. Everything in nature must obey my orders." But his courtiers and subjects did not believe his words at all. The king was determined to prove his power. One morning, he took his courtiers to a seashore where sea waves were rolling one after another. The waves lashed at the feet of the king as usual. The king ordered the waves to move back, but they hardly paid heed to his words. Instead, seeing a large wave approaching him, the king moved back in fear. The foolish king realized that nature was more powerful than he and others.

Pride brings nothing but foolishness and dejection in reality

(41) Use the following hints to Write a story of about 100 words. Give the story a suitable title.

[**Hints:** a farmer finds a snake almost dead with cold—brings it home—warms it—saves its life—the snake is about to bite the farmer's son—the farmer chases the snake away.]

An Ungrateful Snake

Once, a farmer lived in a village with his wife and five-year-old son. Returning home one winter day, he found a nearly dead snake lying beside the road. The farmer felt pity for it, so he took it home, warmed it, and fed it, saving its life. Another day, the farmer's son unknowingly entered the room where the snake was kept. Upon seeing the boy, the snake was about to bite him, but the farmer intervened and chased the snake away from his house.

Ungrateful hardly pay tributes

(42) Carefully read the points given below, and write a paragraph using them:

(a hungry dog—in search of food—got a piece of bone from a butcher's shop—crossing a bridge over narrow river—found another dog with a bone under water—barked and lose his piece too in the water.)

Greedy Dog

Once upon a time, a starving dog wandered in search of food. He found a juicy bone and felt very happy at a butcher's shop. He took the bone and ran towards a bridge over a river. Upon seeing his reflection in the water, he mistook it for another dog with a bone. Desiring the bone, he barked at the reflection, causing the bone to fall into the water as he opened his mouth. He ended up losing his bone.

(43) See the picture. Has any idea come to mind? Now, study the points given and develop them into a story. (However, the story has been extracted from Aesop's Fables):

The Hare and the Tortoise

Once upon a time, a tortoise and a hare lived in a forest. They were good friends. The tortoise was known for his slow speed, while the hare was proud of his fast speed and often made fun of his friend's slowness. One day, the tortoise challenged the hare to a race, and the hare agreed instantly. A horse was selected as the referee.

The race started, and the hare ran fast, reaching far ahead of the tortoise. As he came to a large tree by a lake, he decided to nap, thinking he could still easily win. Meanwhile, the tortoise steadily made his way and passed the sleeping hare, almost reaching the finishing point.
Upon waking up and realizing the tortoise was close to winning, the hare dashed towards the finishing point, but it was too late! The slow but steady tortoise had already crossed the finishing line, and the horse declared him the winner of the race.

Moral: 'Slow but Steady wins the race.

(44) Read the picture series carefully and develop them into a story. Write a moral to it.

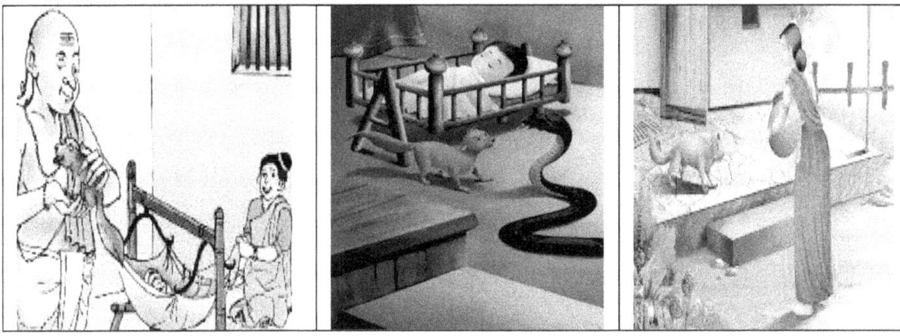

The Mongoose and the Brahmin's Wife

A Brahmin, his wife, and his baby boy lived in a small village. They had a pet mongoose who lived with them. One day, the brahmin was out of chores as usual. His wife left the baby in the cradle and fetched water from a nearby well. She asked the mongoose to take care of the baby while she was away. The mongoose began to guard the baby. After some time, the mongoose could see a snake crawling into the house. The mongoose rushed to the snake, attacked it, and in the fight the snake was killed. The mongoose was happy it could save the life of the baby. After some time, the Brahmin's wife entered the house with a pot of water. She saw a mongoose with blood all over its mouth. The lady was terrified at the sight and assumed that the mongoose had killed the baby. Furious, the lady dropped the pot of water on the mongoose and beat it to death with a stick. Then she went inside and found the baby sleeping safely in the cradle. The lady realized what she had done and repented for her acting.

Moral: Do not act in haste without understanding the situation.

(45) Read the picture and the following points, develop them into a story, and write a moral for them.

Four Friends and a Hunter

Once upon a time, a deer, a turtle, a crow, and a rat were good friends who lived happily in a jungle. One day, the deer got caught in a hunter's trap, so the friends devised a plan to save him. The deer pretended to be in pain and then lay still, appearing as if it were dead. The crow and the other birds sat on the deer and started pecking at it as they would with a dead animal. At the same time, the turtle crossed the hunter's path to distract him. The hunter, thinking the deer was dead, went after the turtle. While the hunter was distracted, the rat chewed open the net to free the deer, and the crow picked up the turtle and swiftly moved it away from the hunter.

Moral: Teamwork can achieve great results.

(46) Read the points and develop them into a story. Write also the title and a moral to the story. [Cap seller – going to market – felt tired – slept under a tree – woke up to see caps missing from the basket– looked up in wonder – monkeys wearing caps – tried several methods– failed – out of frustration, threw his cap – monkeys too threw theirs –collected, and went away happily.]

A Cap Seller and Some Monkeys

A cap seller was on his way to the market. Feeling tired, he decided to take a nap under a tree. When he woke up, he noticed that the caps from his basket were missing. To his amazement, he looked up and saw monkeys wearing his caps. The cap seller attempted various methods to retrieve his caps from the monkeys, but all his efforts failed. Frustrated, he threw his cap on the ground, which led the monkeys to do the same. Seizing the opportunity, the cap seller collected the caps and happily went on his way.

Moral of the Story: Sometimes, thinking creatively and finding a peaceful solution can lead to a positive outcome.

(47) Read the points and develop them into a story. Write also the title and a moral to the story. [An Arab has a camel— Arab sleeps inside a tent— Camel Shivers outside— Arab agrees to let the camel put its neck inside— then its forelegs— camel enters the tent and pushes the Arab outside.]

An Arab and His Camel

An Arab owned a camel. One chilly night, as the Arab was sleeping snugly inside his tent, he noticed his camel shivering in the cold outside. Filled with compassion, the Arab allowed the camel to put its neck inside the tent to keep warm. However, taking advantage of the Arab's kindness, the camel slowly but steadily maneuvered into the tent, eventually forcing the Arab out into the cold night air.

Don't let your kindness be your Weakness to others

(48) Read the points and develop them into a story. Write also the title and a moral to the story. [A woodcutter—cutting wood —axe fell in a pond —started weeping —God appeared — asked—brought a golden axe—wood cutter denied —brought a silver axe — not accepted —brought an iron axe —stretched his hand —pleased with his honesty—gifted the golden and silver axes.]

An Honest Woodcutter

Once upon a time, a woodcutter was busy cutting wood when his axe fell into a pond. Distraught, he started weeping. Suddenly, God appeared before him and asked what had happened. The woodcutter explained, and God offered to help by bringing out a golden axe. The woodcutter, being honest, denied that it was his. God brought out a silver axe, but the woodcutter again denied it. Finally, God brought out an iron axe, which was indeed the woodcutter's. Impressed by the woodcutter's honesty, God gifted him the golden and silver axes.

"Honesty is always rewarded."

(49) Read the points and develop them into a story. Write also the title and a moral to the story. [A father and a son — going to market with a donkey — son sits on a donkey —someone asked the son to make his father sit on the donkey—another advised to ride both together— other said, 'inhuman!'—' why not carry the donkey on your shoulders?'

A Father, Son, and a Donkey

A father and his son were on their way to the market with their donkey. The son was sitting on the donkey when someone advised him to let his father sit on the donkey instead. Then, another person suggested that they both should ride the donkey. However, within minutes, a man noticed it. He criticized them, saying making the donkey carry their weight was inhuman. He suggested that they should take the donkey on their shoulders to the market.

Listen to everybody, but follow your judgment.

(50) Read the points and develop them into a story. Write also the title and a moral to the story. [A captive escaped from king's cell—soldiers came after him in a forest—a lion, roaring in pain—its paw was swollen—the captive approached, removed the thorn—soon he was arrested—took him to the king— the king ordered him to be thrown before a hungry lion—a lion rushed towards—recognized its savior—licked his feet—left the king and others amazed—King came to know the reason —set him free, a kind-hearted and honest man to be.]

A Lion and a Kind Captive

Sample 1

An escaped prisoner, running for his life, was relentlessly pursued by a group of soldiers deep into a dense and mysterious forest. As he desperately tries to elude his captors, he stumbles upon a majestic lion with a thorn embedded in its swollen paw. Overcoming his initial fear, the captive carefully approaches the lion and removes the thorn, alleviating the animal's pain.

Soon the captive was arrested by the soldiers. He was brought before the formidable king. Without hesitation, the king ordered that the captive be thrown into a pit with a fierce and famished lion as punishment for his escape.

Miraculously, as the prisoner was pushed into the pit, the ferocious lion approached him, but to everyone's astonishment, it didn't attack. Instead, the lion nuzzled the captive, revealing a bond that defied explanation. The king, witnessing this remarkable scene, was moved by the unexpected turn of events and came to a profound realization. Recognizing the captive's true nature as a compassionate and genuinely good-hearted individual, the king immediately ordered his release and bestowed upon him the highest honor.

Sample 2

An escaped captive was pursued by soldiers into a forest, where he encountered a lion with a swollen paw. The captive removed the thorn from the lion's paw, but soon, he was arrested by the king's soldiers. He was brought before the king. The king ordered the captive to be thrown before a hungry lion, which surprisingly recognized him as its savior. The king, amazed by this, set the captive free, identifying him as a kind-hearted and honest man.

Kindness is always rewarded

(51) Read the points and develop them into a story. Write also the title and a moral to the story. [King Midas had a thirst for more gold—a fairy appeared— "gold, more gold at every hour"—'So, let it be,' said the fairy— 'Whatever you touch' —the fairy disappeared—Midas's excitement knew no bound—began to touch everything at hand—castle turned to golden castle—Midas, pleased —Midas got hungry — could not eat —the prince ran towards his father— Midas, in love, forgot about the fairy's blessing—his son turned to gold— Midas realized—prayed to take away his golden touch.]

The Golden Touch

Once, there was a wealthy king named Midas, but his thirst for more gold was insatiable. One day, a fairy appeared and asked him what he desired. In his greed, Midas asked for more gold every hour. The fairy granted his wish, saying that everything he would touch would turn to gold.

Midas was ecstatic and touched everything in the palace. In seconds, everything began to turn into gold. Over time, he felt hungry. He touched his food, and it turned into gold. His joy soon turned to despair out of hunger. Eventually, his little son entered his room. Out of love, the king took him on his shoulders. Alas! His beloved son turned into gold. Panicked, the king began to blame his indomitable avarice. He realized his foolishness. Midas prayed to the fairy to take away his golden touch.

Moral: Greed leads to sorrow, and true wealth lies in the things that cannot be bought with gold.

About Author

Mr. Peter is a professional teacher and author of numerous academic books on English Grammar and Writing Skills. Additionally, he has authored various works, including stories, novels, and poems. Some of his works also collaborate with Mr. Sarkar and others, authors from Bharat (formerly India). Mr. Peter's books have been published through global platforms such as Amazon, Notion Press, Flipkart, and Google following their release. These books are accessible on Amazon Kindle, Google Play Store, and Google Books in various formats like eBooks, audiobooks, Paperback, and Hardcover. To locate his works, one can search by the book title or author's name on the web browsers and platforms mentioned.
Thank you—best of Luck.

Some important works by the writer & Co-author:

1. Study of Nouns, Pronouns, Adjectives & Articles (detail study) ISBN: 979-832-697-263-7 / 979-832-697-510-2
2. All about Verbs (Forms, Functions, Conjugation, Tense, Voice Change, Forming Questions & Negation) ISBN: 979-832-807-531-2 / 979-832-807-688-3
3. Study of Adverbs, Prepositions, Conjunctions & Interjections ISBN: 979-832-886-943-0 / 979-883-987-196-0
4. Detail Study of Phrases, Clauses & Sentences, including Idioms & Phrasal Verbs ISBN: 979-832-939-104-6 / 979-884-011-097-3
5. Study of Subject-Verb Agreement, Narration Change, and Use of Punctuation, including Analysis, Synthesis, & Split-up (Study through charts, division, explanation, and examples) ISBN: 979-880-723-013-3 / 979-888-704-674-7
6. **Peter's 'English Grammar, A Complete Version of English Grammar,** (detail study, explanation & examples)ISBN: 979-879-725-020-3 / 979-888-704-463-7
7. **Question Bank of English Grammar & Composition**(Learn through Exercises) ISBN: 979-883-531-890-2 / 979-888-733-132-4
8. **Rhetoric & Prosody**(A handbook of Figures of Speech, rhymes, feet of poetic lines for High School Students) ISBN: 979-840-526-645-9 / 979-888-684-952-3
9. **A Book of Advanced Writing Skill, the Complete Version**(incl Part-1, 2 & 3) ISBN: 979-836-472-826-5 / 979-888-869-835-8
10. **English *Grammar* & Question Bank Together** For Class VI to XII (Learn through Exercise) ISBN 979-838-571-382 0
11. **New English Pal,** Class **10** (A Complete Guide Book for Smart Learning, based on WBBSE syllabus) by **P. Sarkar, based on Peter's Grammar and Composition**: [Separate book for each class from 5 to 10]
12. **The Rainbow** (A Collection of Short Stories) ISBN 10: 979-832141310-4; 979-832141545-0 & ISBN 13: 979-889363024-4

Author page URL's:
https://www.amazon.com/author/mr.peter
https://www.amazon.in/~/e/B09QW2P4TY(Bharat/India)
https://www.amazon.co.uk/~/e/B09QW2P4TY
https://www.amazon.de/~/e/B09QW2P4TY
https://www.amazon.fr/~/e/B09QW2P4TY
https://www.amazon.co.jp/~/e/B09QW2P4TY
https://www.amazon.es/~/e/B09QW2P4TY
https://www.amazon.it/~/e/B09QW2P4TY
https://www.amazon.com.br/kindle-dbs/entity/author?asin=B09QW2P4TY

In Bharat/India, you can purchase the paperback version of my book by visiting notionpress.com and typing the author's name or title of a book in the search box. You may also use these links:
https://www.facebook.com/groups/mr.peter
https://notionpress.com/store/s?NP_Books%5Bquery%5D=Mr.+Peter
https://notionpress.com/store/s?NP_Books%5Bquery%5D=P.+Sarkar

The Following Coupons can be applied on **notionpress.com** till the end of the coupons:

Coupon Codes	**Book Name**	**Buy for**	**Discount %**	**Rebate Prices**
Bulk13	Study of Nouns, Pronouns, Adjectives & Articles (detail study)	2 & more	52	~~300~~ 144
Bulk14	All about Verbs (Forms, Functions, Conjugation, Tense, Voice Change, Forming Questions & Negation)	2 & more	50	~~420~~ 210
~~PujaDeal3 / Deal3~~	Study of Adverbs, Prepositions, Conjunctions & Interjections	1 & more	~~20 & 26~~	290
Bulk15	Detail Study of Phrases, Clauses & Sentences, including Idioms & Phrasal Verbs	2 & more	52	~~290~~ 136
~~PujaDeal5 / Deal5~~	Study of Subject-Verb Agreement, Narration Change, Use of Punctuation; including Analysis, Synthesis & Split-up	1 & more	~~20 & 26~~	310
PujaDeal6 / Deal7	Question Bank of English Grammar & Composition	1 & more	20 & 28	~~559~~ 448 & 403
PujaDeal7 / Deal8/ bulk11	Rhetoric & Prosody	1 & more	20, 26 & 55	~~240~~ 192, 178 &108
PujaDeal8 / Deal9	Steps to Composition (Development of Writing Skill, from Primary to Secondary Level, Part-1)	1 & more	20 & 26	~~300~~ 240 & 222
PujaDeal9 / Deal10	Development of Writing Skill, Part-2	1 & more	18 & 24	~~365~~ 300 & 278
PujaDeal10 / Deal11	Development of Writing Skill, Part-3	1 & more	18 & 24	~~365~~ 300 & 278
unique00 / bulk00	A Book of Advanced Writing Skill, the Complete Version (incl. Part-1, 2 & 3)	1 & more	15 & 23	~~780~~ 663 & 601
unique01 / bulk1/bulk10	Peter's 'English Grammar' (Complete Version of English Grammar)	1 & more	23, 30 & 48	~~1201~~ 925, 841 & 625
unique02/bulk 02	English Grammar & Question Bank Together	1 & more	30 & 48	~~690~~ 483 & 359
spl01 / bulk04	New English Pal, Class 9 (based on WBBSE syllabus)	1 & more	35 & 47	~~490~~ 319 & 260
spl02 / bulk05	New English Pal, Class 10 (based on WBBSE syllabus)	1 & more	34 & 47	~~480~~ 317 & 255
spl03 / bulk06	New English Pal, Class 5 (based on WBBSE syllabus)	1 & more	29 & 52	~~280~~ 199 & 134
spl04 / bulk07	New English Pal, Class 8 (based on WBBSE syllabus)	1 & more	30 & 46	~~420~~ 294 & 227
spl05 / bulk08	New English Pal, Class 7 (based on WBBSE syllabus)	1 & more	30 & 54	~~400~~ 280 & 184
spl06 / bulk09	New English Pal, Class 6 (based on WBBSE syllabus)	1 & more	30 & 56	~~320~~ 224 & 141
spl07 / bulk12	The Rainbow (A Collection of Short Stories)	1 & more	56 & 56	~~299~~ 132 & 132
Note: For Copies of More Than One, Select The 2nd Coupon Given In Each Row of The First Column				

www.ingramcontent.com/pod-product-compliance
Ingram Content Group UK Ltd.
Pitfield, Milton Keynes, MK11 3LW, UK
UKHW060116010826
14089UKWH00003B/13